A HISTORY

GARSTANG &

RAILWAY

GARSTANG AND KNOT END RAILWAY.—Share capital, £60,000, in 6,000 shares, £10 each.—A deposit of 5s. per share to be made on application, which will be returned less the actual disbursements in Parliament, should the application for the act prove unsuccessful during the present session of Parliament. Commencing at the Port of Fleetwood, this line will pass through Preesall, Pilling, Cogie Hill, Nateby, Garstang, and join the London and North Western (Lancaster and Preston), the course of the line (10½ miles in length), is mostly level, and entirely free from engineering difficulties, the result being that it will be unusually cheap to construct. The ancient market town of Garstang has hitherto been virtually without railway communication. It claims to possess the cheapest market in Lancashire for agricultural produce. The resources of the country on each side of the railway are very large, and it is confidentially anticipated that the traffic from the resources of the locality alone will pay nearly five per cent. upon the capital, after allowing for working expenses. Independently of local traffic, arising from agricultural produce, it is expected that the receipts from the imports of cattle, flax, provisions, &c., into the Wyre, and the general interchange of commodities between Ireland and the manufacturing districts will be large. Passengers from Scotland, and the North of England, on their way to Fleetwood, Blackpool, &c., would effect a saving of 20 miles by the use of this route.—*Welch's Circular.*

Preston Herald 2 January 1864

ROBERT CUNLIFFE

The History of the Garstang & Knott End Railway.

Published 2017 by Robert Cunliffe

Copyright © 2017 Robert Cunliffe

ISBN 978-0-244-32459-9

Introduction

The aim of this book is to chronologically relate the history of the Garstang Knott End Railway with an emphasis on the history of the line and places without straying too much to the technical side. Extensive use of contempo local press reports are used. An excellent book by Robert Rush and Martin Price (published in 1964 and a new edition in 1985) covers the technical det of the line and the engines and includes details of the locomotives and rollin stock. This book explores the history of the area as well as the timeline of the railway story with an emphasis on the surviving visible signs and route of the line. A lot of the illustrations are modern day photographs together with older maps showing the route. There are some old postcard illustrations and some modern paintings.

Garstang Art's Centre. Garstang Town Station ran to the rear when this was the Grammar School. Painting by Glenda Cunliffe

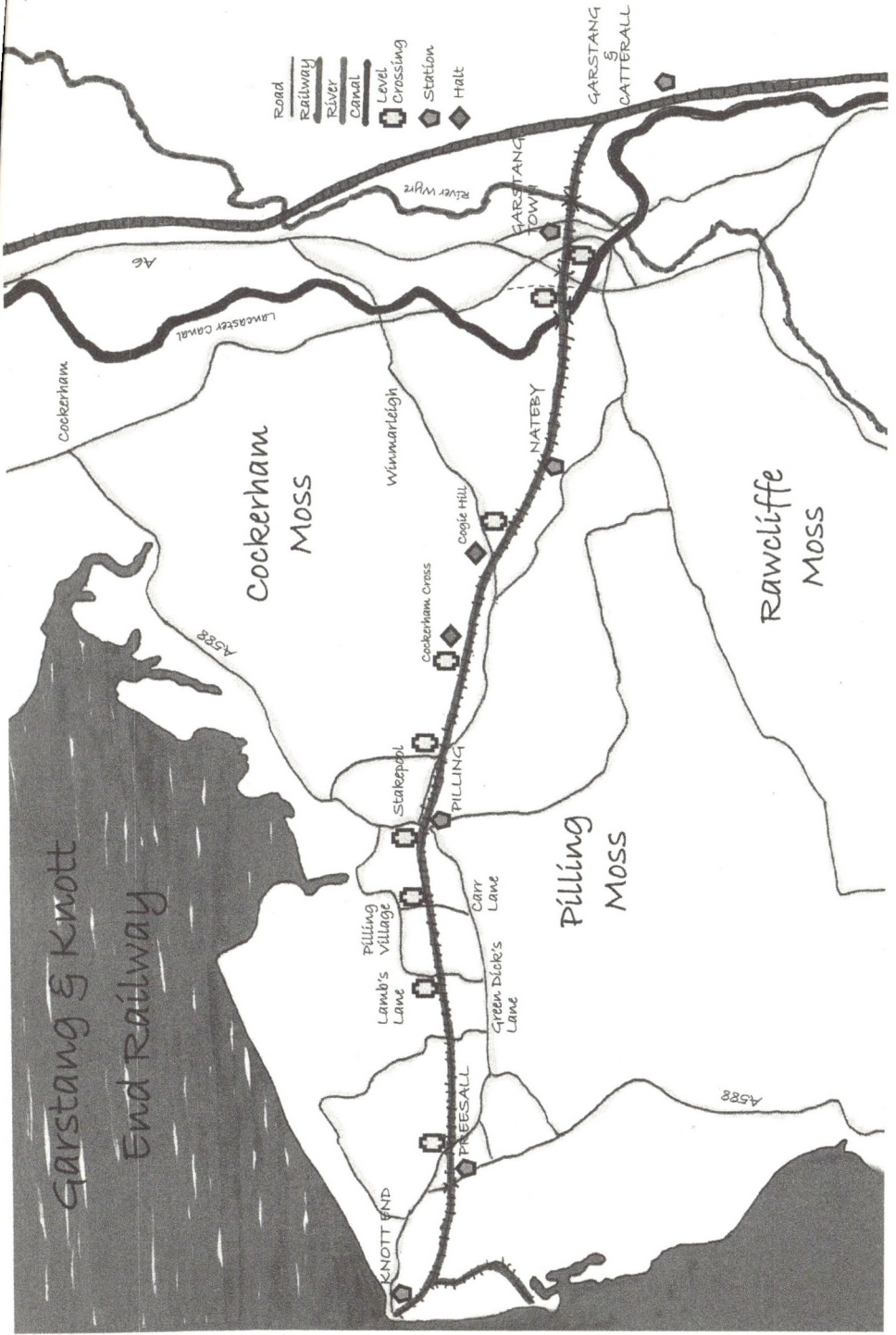

Hand drawn map of the route by the author (not to scale)

Chronology of G&KER

Prospectus issued December 1863.

House of Commons committee meeting, 27 April 1864.

House of Lords committee meeting, 16 June 1864.

Sanctioned by Act of Parliament 30 June 1864.

First contractor, Wheatley Kirk, of Manchester, resigns, April 1865.

Appeal to Parliament for an extension of time until 1870, May 1867.

It was decided that the four and a half miles of line between Pilling and Knott End should not be built for the time being, December 1867.

Appeal to Parliament for a further 12 month extension, June 1870.

The Garstang Rolling Stock Company was formed, 12 October 1870

Opened 5 December 1870.

Ceremonial opening 14 December 1870.

Ceased operation in early April 1872.

Reopened for goods traffic 23 February 1875.

Passengers 17 April 1875.

The Garstang & Knott End Railway Engine Company formed, 9 December 1875.

The Garstang Rolling Stock Company was formerly dissolved by a notice in the London Gazette, 15 January 1884.

The Garstang & Knott End Railway Engine Company final meeting, 12 October 1898.

Prospectus issued October 1898.

Knott End Railway Company formed by Act Royal Assent, 12 August 1898.

First Sod Cut 25 January 1899 by Sir M White Ridley M.P.

Contract let to Worthington, of Dublin, 1 Jan 1908.

The Garstang & Knot End Railway and the Knott End Railway were merged by Act of Parliament 18 June 1908

Line completed to Knott End 29 July 1908.

New halt opened at Carr Lane to the west of Pilling, 1911

New halt opened to the east of Pilling 1911

A short branch of one and a half miles laid to the United Alkali Company works near Preesall, 1912.

Became part of LMS in 1923.

Withdrew passenger service 31 March 1930.

Final train 29 March 1930

Line closed beyond Pilling in 1950

Line cut back to Garstang Town 1963

Closed to all traffic August 1965.

LOCAL EXCURSION BOOKINGS

NOTICE.

On and after FRIDAY, July 31st, during AUGUST and SEPTEMBER, 1908, CHEAP

Excursion Bookings

Will be issued every day, as under, by any Train leaving KNOTT END, GARSTANG, or GARSTANG and CATTERALL JUNCTION, between the hours of 11-0 a.m. and 6-0 p.m., and by all Trains on SUNDAYS and BANK HOLIDAYS.

RETURN FARES:

Knott End to Pilling - - -	6d.
Knott End to Nateby - - -	10d.
Knott End to Garstang - - -	1/-
Knott End to Garstang & Catterall Junc.	1/3
Preesall to Nateby - - - -	10d.
Preesall to Garstang - - -	1/-
Preesall to Garstang & Catterall Junc.	1/3
Pilling to Knott End - - -	6d.
Pilling to Garstang & Catterall Junction	9d.
Nateby to Preesall or Knott End -	10d.
Garstang to Preesall or Knott End -	1/-
Garstang and Catterall Junc. to Pilling	9d.
Garstang and Catterall Junction to Preesall or Knott End -	1/3

G. ERROLL WORTHINGTON

General Manager.

Printed at the GAZETTE NEWS Offices, Blackpool and Fleetwood.

Garstang History

Garstang is an old market town within the Wyre Borough of Lancashire. It is midway between Preston and Lancaster on the A6 road. The Lancaster Canal goes through the centre of the town as does the River Wyre. The M6 and The West Coast Main Line are to the east of the town. There is now no railway station. The population of the parish in the 2011 census was 4,268 and in the larger Garstang built up area was 6,779. The town is overlooked by the ruins of Greenhalgh Castle built in 1490 by Thomas Stanley. There is a Thursday street market and a small market hall on Wednesdays to Saturdays.

There are now three excerpts from books published at different times to give a flavour of the view of Garstang before, during and after the construction of the Garstang to Knott End Railway (for most of the construction period this was spelt Knot End).

Pigot and Co's Commercial Directory of Lancashire 1828-9.

"Garstang, a market town and parish, in the hundred and deanery of Amounderness, and in the archdeacoury of Richmond, is 228 miles from London, 42 miles from Manchester, 20 miles from Chorley, 11 from Lancaster and Preston, and 10 from Kirkham. Its ancient appellation was Gayrsteng, supposed to be a Saxon personal name. The town is situated on the western banks of the river Wyre, on the great western north road from London to Edinburgh, and derives considerable advantage from the continual passing of different vehicles and travellers through it. Garstang was first incorporated in the seventh year of Edward II., its charter placing the government of the town in the hands of a bailiff and seven capital burgesses, who are empowered to try misdemeanours within the borough. The parish church, dedicated to St Helen stands a mile and a half from the town, in the township of Kirkland, and in that part of the parish called Garstang Church town. It is a vicarage, in the incumbency of the Rev. John Pedder, sen. The other places of worship are, a chapel of ease, and one each for the independents, catholics and methodists. The free grammar school educates six boys, who are nominated by the corporation, and the catholic school instructs twenty poor children. The present lord of the manor is Frederick Kepple Esq., of Lexham Hall, in Norfolk, who holds, by his stewards, two courts in the year. Within a quarter of a mile south of the principle street, the Lancaster canal crosses the Wyre by a beautiful aqueduct, and upon the banks of that river are cotton, corn and flax mills. The weekly market is on Thursday, and there are cattle markets on the alternate Thursday between the first Thursday in Lent and Holy Thursday. The fairs are on Holy Thursday, 10th July, and 22nd November. In 1821 Garstang parish contained 7,403 persons."

The next extract is from

Northwards by A Hewitson published in 1900

"The River Wyre runs between the townships of Barnacre with Bonds and Garstang. It takes its rise in the lonely, wide spreading hills at the head of Wyresdale; and from its source, in the wild, high region named, to its debouchure, at Fleetwood, into Lune Deep, the course of it is a very crooked, wandering character. Michael Drayton, in his "Polyolbion" (published 1612-22), gives a graphic, compactly picturesque description of the Wyre. He refers to it as;

Arising but a Rill at first from Wyersdales lap,

Yet still receiving her strength from her full Mothers pap.

As downe to Seaward she, her serious course doth ply,

Takes Caldor coming in, to beare her company,

From Woolscrags (Wolf Crag's) cliffy foot, a Hill to her at hand,

By that fayre Forrest known, within her verge to stand.

So Bowland from her breast sends Brock her to attend

As she a Forrest is, so likewise doth she send

Her Child, on Wyresdales Flood, the dainty Wyre to wayt,

With her assisting Rills, when Wyre is once repleat;

Shoe in her crooked course to Seaward softly slides,

Where Pillins (Pilling's) mighty Mosse, and Mertons (Marton's), on her sides.

Their boggy breast out lay, and Skipton (Skipool) downe doth crawl

To entertaine this Wyer, attained to her fall.

It is conjectured that the original bridge over the Wyre between Bonds and Garstang was built near the end of the fifteenth century, by the Earl of Derby, for the purpose of securing communication with Greenhalgh Castle. Owing to its inconvenient formation, it was high and very narrow, this bridge was pulled down and the present one erected in its place about the year 1750. A stone at the termination of the parapet of the bridge (north east end) bears the inscription, "J Threlfall, B.M. 1829." On both sides of the bridge, at the Garstang end, there appears to have been an addition of several yards made to the parapet of the original structure. The record at present in the County Bridgemaster's office, at Preston, respecting this bridge, does not go as far back as 1829; but the presumption is that a parapet was extended in that year, when a person named J Threlfall was the bridgemaster. Just below the bridge there is the weir of Bonds corn mill, and this by its back watering influence causes the Wyre here to be broad and somewhat deep. As soon as Wyre Bridge is crossed, northwards, the town of Garstang is entered.

In the Doomsday Book Garstang is designated "Cherestanc," the land area of it, or connected with it, being "six carucates."

In other records,etc, not so old the name appears variously as Geirstanke, Gairestang, Gairstang, Gayrestang, Gairstange, Garstrenge,Garstrang, Garsting and Garstang.

Early in the thirteenth century the manor of Garstang belonged to the Lancastres, Barons of Kendal and Wyresdale. Agnes, widow of William de Lancastre, the third baron, held the manor as her dower about the middle of the same century. Two nephews, Peter de Brus and Walter de Lindsey, afterwards became possessed of it. Subsequently the manor was owned by the Lindseys. Sir John Haverington, of Farleton, near Kirkby Lonsdale, was, during the latter part of the fourteenth century, the owner of the manor or of certain property in it, through marriage. Proprietary rights in Garstang were then successively exercised by Henry Duke of Lancaster, and a descendant, the Multons descendants of the de Lancastre family, one or more of the Twenge family, Sir William de Mollineux, the de Coucy de Gynes, the Rigmadens, etc. In 1535-36 the manor became the property of the Crown. Afterwards, with certain reservations on behalf of the tenants, it went to the Savoy Hospital, in London. The manor next passed, by lease, successively, to Henry Saville, his servant William Saville, William Holden, the Rigmadens and the Gerards. In 1738 the manor reverted to the Crown. In 1742 it was granted to Mr William Hall of the Middle Temple, London, for a term of 30 years. Later, in the same year, the Hon. Edward Walpole obtained the manor for the remainder of the term, and soon afterwards, the King, by Act of Parliament, conveyed to him-with the view of giving encouragement to the trade of Garstang and providing security for improvements made therein- the manor in fee; and a descendant of his, by marriage (Mr Bertram William Arnold-Keppel, who resides near Swaffham, in Nofolk), is now lord of the manor, and owns the major portion of the property in Garstang. The town of Garstang was incorporated by a charter, granted in the reign of Edward II (1314). This charter was surrendered to Charles II, and renewed by him on August 5th, 1680. By this renewed charter the town was made a "free Burrough;" its governing body consisting of a Bailiff and seven Burgesses, and locally designated in after years " the Mayor and Corporation of Garstang."

The November cattle fair at Garstang used to be a very large one. For instance at the fair in 1805 there were, from the North alone, nearly 3,000 cattle; at that in 1814, there were 2,300; and at the fair in 1821, in addition to a large number of English cattle there were between 2,000 and 3,000 head of Scots. Formerly there was a fair or market for cheese at Garstang. William Stout, a Lancaster Quaker, and tradesman, says in his diary that in 1691-2 he "went to Preston fair, principally to buy cheese; the market for cheese then being mostly at Garstang and Preston." Another writer observes-an abundance of potatoes are raised about the place and sent to London, Ireland and Scotland." Potatoe growing, to the point of " abundance," is still a characteristic of the district, especially on the west-ward side.

In the old coaching days Garstang came in for a large measure of patronage, and was a particularly well known place. Being on the great north-west highway between London and Edinburgh, all the coaches which ran on this road were pulled up for passenger refreshments, horse changing, etc, at Garstang. Not unfrequently, also, some of the passengers who had travelled a long distance broke their journey on reaching Garstang, stayed all night, taking advantage of such hotel accommodation as the old place provided for persons of their order. William Black, the novelist, made a halt at Garstang in 1871, and some of the incidents in one of his best stories have their venue at the Royal Oak, in the old town, and along the banks of the Wyre, etc, in the neighbourhood.

About 1836, when the survey was being made for the Preston and Lancaster railway, much indifference, if not even a strong aversion, to the project was shown in Garstang by either the inhabitants or the family owning the town; and it is said that in consequence of this the present route of the railway, on the eastern side-a mile distant, as the crow flies, and nearly two miles off by the ordinary road, from Garstang, was adopted.

The "Market Place" of Garstang is a sort of triangular space in front of the Royal Oak Hotel, and in the centre of this space is the old Market Cross-a far worn stone pillar, on a stone base. A small metal plate, fixed on one side of the pedestal, bears an inscription to the effect that the Cross was repaired by public subscription, in 1897, in commemoration of the Queen's Jubilee (The Diamond Jubilee which occurred in the year named). Originally, the column would, no doubt, be surmounted by a cross-hence the name Market Cross. The number of public houses open is 10, namely, the Royal Oak, Golden Ball, King's Arms, Eagle and Child, the Horns, Pack Horse, Crown, Brown Cow, Wheat Sheaf, and Farmer's Arms. Over the front door of the Brown Cow there is the date 1685.

St Thomas's Church, Garstang, is the successor of a chapel-of-ease, originally licensed for divine service in 1437. The Plundered Ministers' Committee ordered, in 1646, an annual payment of £50 out of the tithe profits of the impropriate rectory of Goosnargh, sequestered from Sir Thomas Tildesley, "delinquent," for the "maintenance of a minister at the chappell of the Market Towne of Garstange," and subsequently the same committee ordered the sum of £50 to be allowed and paid out of impropriate tithes arising within the parish of Kirkham, sequestered from Thomas Clifton Esq., "papist and delinquent, to and for the maintenance of such minister as shall be approved of by the classis" of the county of Lancaster, to officiate in the said "chappell." This place of worship was rebuilt in 1666, and again in 1796, whilst in 1876 it was restored and enlarged. It has been a parish church, in accordance with the provisions of the Blanford Act, since 1880, in which year a separate district, taken out of the civil parish of Garstang, was assigned to it.

From the Garstang and Catterall Station-the station of the Preston and Lancaster (now L&NW) Railway-there is a junction line to Garstang, and thence westward to Pilling. This line, called the Garstang & Knot End Railway, was opened for traffic on the 5th December, 1870. Originally, it was intended to form a section of quite a big affair: its western

Ruins of Greenhalgh Castle. The G&KER ran closely by.

terminus had to be at Knot End, opposite Fleetwood; there had to be docks at Knot End to secure coasting business, particularly in connection with Ireland, and for certain American trade, etc; the line had to go eastwards as far as Hull, or run into some railway having a direct route to that seaport, and at the first open meeting in support of the project, a meeting held at the Royal Oak Inn, Garstang, a wonderfully fine picture of prospective traffic and dividend earning was drawn."

The Royal Oak Hotel and the Market Cross

The Bridge over the River Wyre

The third extract is from

The Victoria County History of 1912.

The parish of Garstang has an area of 28,881 acres, and the population in 1901 numbered 5,896, employed for the most part in agriculture, though there are some scattered factories.

The northern boundary is peculiar, Holleth being quite detached from the main body of the parish and having a small part of its area within the parish of Cockerham, in which also is contained about three fourths of Cleveley. Some evidences of the Roman occupation have been found. Before the Conquest only three manors existed, Garstang, Catterall and Claughton, and these three, with the addition of Bilsborrow, were all the townships existing in 1327-41. It was only slowly that the other townships became separate. In 1624 the county lay was apportioned as follows: Garstang, £10 5s. 3¼d.; Catterall, £1 13s. 7¾d.; Claughton, 18s. 9¾d.; and Bilsborrow, £1 4s. 6¼d., making a total contribution of £14 2s. 3d. towards the £100 levied upon the hundred. The older fifteenth was of similar proportions. The townships had by that time become distinct, and Bishop Gastrell in 1717 reckoned them as eleven, arranged in four quarters, Garstang, Claughton, Barnacre and Wyresdale; Pilling was in the first-named quarter.

Garstang is midway between Preston and Lancaster, on the ancient road to Scotland, and has thus witnessed many stirring events, such as the devastating raid by the Scots in 1322, but ancient remains are scanty.

There was a visitation of the plague in 1349–50. In 1444 William Marsden and others were charged with having broken into a fulling mill at Garstang and stolen forty ells of woollen cloth called russet, value 40s., the goods of John Ingoll.

Leland, journeying north about 1535, says: 'After I rode over Brock water, rising a vi miles off in the hills on the right hand and goeth at last into Wyre. Calder rising about the same hills, goeth also into Wyre; I rode over it. By the town's end of Garstang I rode over a great stone bridge on Wyre ere I came to it. Wyre rises a viii or ten miles from Garstang out of the hills on the right hand and cometh by Greenhalgh, a pretty castle of the lord of Derby's, and more than half a mile thence to Garstang in Amounderness. Some saith that Garstang was a market town.

The district was hostile to the Reformation and favourable to the king's cause in the Civil War though some companies were raised for the other side. Greenhalgh Castle was one of the two important fortresses remaining till 1645 to give trouble to the Parliamentarians. Their historian gives the following account of its surrender:—

Colonel Dodding with his regiment, with Major Joseph Rigby's companies, laid close siege to Greenhalgh Castle, keeping their main guard at Garstang town, into which [castle] were gotten many desperate Papists. Their governor was one Mr. Anderton. They vexed the country thereabouts extremely, fetching in the night time many honest men from their houses, making a commodity of it. They sallied out oft upon the Leaguers and killed some. They stood it out stoutly all that winter. The country was put to extraordinary charges in maintaining the northern men, who made a prey without pity, such abundance of provision they weekly destroyed. The Leaguers had thought to have undermined the castle and blown it up with gunpowder, and great cost was spent about it to pioneers, but to no effect; the ground was so sandy it would not stand. At last this Anderton died, and them there within being thereby discouraged, they were glad to come to a composition to deliver it up upon conditions—which were, that they might go to their own houses and be safe. It was ordered that the castle should be demolished and made untenable and all the timber taken out of it and sold, which was done. And so it lies ruinated. . . . It was very strong, and builded so that it was thought impregnable with any ordnance whatsoever, having but one door into it, and the walls of an exceeding thickness and very well secured together.

Celia Fiennes, who passed through this 'little market town' about 1700, was here 'first presented with the clap bread which is much talked of, made all of oats.

In the Jacobite rising of 1715 the town clerk, Roger Muncaster, joined their forces, as did several others of the district. Muncaster was executed at Preston, and three of the local men at Garstang on 14th February 1715–16. Though Prince Charles Edward and his army passed through in 1745, it does not appear that they secured any adherents in this parish.

A century ago the district was famous for its cattle, which were of a peculiar breed, 'of a smaller size than the Lancashire, of elegant shape and beautifully curled hair, with wide spreading horns and straight backs.' The Wyre then supplied the inhabitants with plenty of fine soft water, and afforded good diversion to the angler as abounding with trout, chub and gudgeon and in springtime with smelts."

Extracts from The Victoria County History of 1912 for Pilling and Preesall

Pilling

"This large township, containing 6,060 acres, is level and lies very low, the highest ground within it scarcely exceeding 25 ft. above sea level. A large part is moss-land, much of which has been reclaimed. A small detached portion lies within Preesall to the west, and another within Cockerham to the north. The principal village lies in the northern end, near the place where the central brook runs into Morecambe Bay, the boundary on that side; in the southern half is a hamlet called Eagland Hill where 33 ft. above sea level is reached; on the border of Upper Rawcliffe lies Eskham. The population in 1901 numbered 1,407.

From the village roads branch out in several directions—to Cockerham, Garstang, St. Michael's, Knott End and the shore of the bay. A single-line railway from Garstang, opened in 1870, has its terminus near the village, from which the connexion with Knott End (for Fleetwood) was completed and opened in 1908.

About half the land is arable, and turf is taken from the moss for fuel.

Damage was, done in 1719 by the sea breaking in. An outbreak of part of the moss near Eskham took place in 1745. A road across the moss called Kate's Pad or the Danes' Pad was made of oak planks resting on sleepers. The local proverb said, 'God's grace and Pilling moss are endless.'

The village was formerly isolated from the rest of the parish by the moss-lands. The road to Preesall and Stalmine was formed in 1780 and that to Garstang was made passable in 1808.

Pilling is not named in Domesday Book, being then, it is supposed, a member of Garstang. It was not granted to the Lancaster family, but retained by the Crown with the hundred, so that it was Theobald Walter who about 1194 granted it as 'the hey of Pilling' to the canons of Cockersand. This grant was confirmed or renewed by King John in 1201, and again by Henry III in 1227. The canons were called upon to prove their title in 1292 and continued to hold Pilling down to the Dissolution In 1543 the Crown sold the grange to John Kechyn or Kitchen of Hatfield, who also acquired parts of the Whalley Abbey estates.

Kitchen settled Pilling or some part of it upon his son John and Grace his wife, but the younger John dying, the widow, in conjunction with her second husband William Hameldon, granted the estate to John Kitchen the father in 1548. Settlements were made in 1557 and 1561,by the former of which a daughter Anne wife of Robert Dalton had Pilling. She died without issue in 1593, having survived her husband, and the heir was her brother Barnaby Kitchen, aged fifty-eight. He died ten years later, leaving three daughters as co-heirs: Alice wife of Hugh Hesketh of North Meols, Anne wife of Thomas Ashton of Croston and Elizabeth wife of Nathaniel Banastre of Altham. A partition was made in 1649, and the manor for over a century descended in thirds.

The Banastre share was in 1678 bought by Edmund Hornby of Poulton, and his descendant, the Rev. Geoffrey Hornby, is stated to have purchased a further share; this part has descended to Mr. Edmund Geoffrey Stanley Hornby of Dalton, near Carnforth. The Heskeths about 1770 seem to have sold their third to the other lords, so that the manor was held in moieties, the Rev. Geoffrey Hornby presenting to the curacy. The Ashton part descended like Croston to the Traffords, and it was afterwards sold. In 1825 the lords of the manor were Edmund Hornby, John Gardner and William Elletson, and in 1850 Edmund Hornby, the owner of the hall, John Gardner and Daniel Elletson. The last-named died in 1856, but had about 1840 sold his share to John Gardner of Sion Hill, Garstang, his brother-in-law, whose son the Rev. John Gardner, LL.D., rector of Skelton 1857–86, succeeded. He bequeathed it to his cousins, the Misses Margaret Jane and Emily Elletson, daughters of Daniel. The advowson of the chapel goes with the lordship. No courts are held. Nothing remains of the old hall.

The canons of Cockersand probably established the chapel of St John the Baptist near their grange when they were placed in possession. Agnes Shepherd had in 1493 the bishop's licence to live a solitary in a cell at Pilling chapel. After the dissolution of the abbey it seems that £2 a year was allowed for the maintenance of a curate, but as this was obviously insufficient it is probable that the chapel was used only irregularly during the latter half of the 16th century. In 1621 some sixty of the inhabitants petitioned the king about the neglect of service, complaining that though they had to pay tithes there was no curate provided. The £2 granted out of the duchy revenues was to be renewed; Sir Robert Bindloss, the lay rector, promised £10 a year from the tithes, the inhabitants were ordered to provide another £8, and the farmer of the demesne £6 13s. 4d. How far this award became operative is uncertain but Mr. Lumley was curate in 1639 and remained there till in the Commonwealth time he was 'silenced' for several misdemeanors. In 1650 the chapel was vacant, and there was no proper maintenance. Early in 1652 it was ordered that £50 a year be paid to the curate out of 'delinquents' estates.

The list of curates shows that the chapel was served regularly from about that time. The certain income in 1717 was £11 13s. 4d. It was then found necessary to build a larger chapel, and the present site was chosen, about a mile west of the old one, for the greater convenience of the inhabitants. This was built in 1717 and consecrated in 1721; it is a small rectangular structure with a bellcot over the west gable. Additional endowments were obtained from Queen Anne's Bounty and other sources. A census of religions was made by the wardens in 1755. They reported 'about 100 families, most in communion of the Church of England, two Protestant Dissenting families, six or eight single persons who are Papists.' A new church was built in 1887, and consists of chancel, clear storied nave with north and south aisles, south porch, and western tower and spire. It is in the Gothic style and the spire forms a prominent landmark. The lords of the manor present alternately. The net value is given as £250."

Preesall

The township is bounded by the River Wyre on the west, the Lune estuary on the north and a small brook on the south. In the north-west angle is the hamlet of Knott End, with a ferry across the Wyre to Fleetwood; to the south, on a stretch of higher land, is Hackinsall; while Preesall lies a mile to the east, on the side of another tract of higher land, and Pilling Lane occupies its north-east corner. The surface to the north and east is flat and lies very low, much of it below the 25 ft. level, but the highest land in the township is about 100 ft. above the sea. There is a wide expanse of sands to the north. The area in all measures 3,393 acres, and there was a population of 1,423 in 1901.

Preesall is the central point of the township; from it roads spread out in various directions-south to Staynall and Stalmine, east towards Garstang and north-west to Knott End. From this last another road goes east along the coast to Pilling. There is a salt mine to the south-west of Preesall, and from it a railway runs down to the Wyre. The railway from Knott End to Pilling and Garstang was opened in 1908. The soil is various, with subsoil of clay and gravel. Wheat, oats and potatoes are grown. Of the land, 869 acres are arable, 1,648 in permanent grass and 20 in woods and plantations. There was a fairy well to the north of Preesall village.

In 1066 Preesall was assessed as six plough-lands and was included in the Preston fee of Earl Tostig. The demesne tithes were in 1094 granted to St. Martin of Sées by Roger of Poitou, and later still, in 1168–9, Preesall was in the demesne of the honour of Lancaster. About 1190 John Count of Mortain granted Preesall and Hackinsall to Geoffrey the Arbalaster or crossbowman, and renewed the gift after he came to the throne. It appears, however, that 4 oxgangs of land in the township had long before been held by serjeanty by Hugh de Hackinsall, whose son Robert obtained confirmations from John when Count of Mortain, and afterwards when king. An agreement respecting the same was made between Geoffrey, as lord of the whole, and Peter de Hackinsall, and, as Geoffrey's descendants assumed their surname from Hackinsall, they no doubt obtained a surrender of the 4 oxgangs.

Geoffrey the Arbalaster held the six plough-lands in 1212 by the service of two crossbows yearly. His son John, known as Arbalaster and de Hackinsall, in 1246 agreed with Eva, his father's widow, as to dower. At the same time he claimed wreck of the sea at Hackinsall, but without good ground. John died in 1262 holding six plough-lands in Hackinsall and Preesall as before, also three plough-lands in Hambleton; Geoffrey his son and heir was of full age. John the son of Geoffrey succeeded before 1284, and was himself followed about 1299 by a brother Richard. John the son of Richard de Hackinsall had a son William, who was in 1335 to marry Alice daughter of John de Bradkirk William had a daughter Ismania, whose daughter Joan married James Pickering, and in 1402 James and Joan had a dispute with the Abbot of Cockersand respecting 900 acres of land in Preesall held by the abbot, a dispute renewed in 1437 by the plaintiff's son James Pickering.

It was probably this James who died in 1479 in possession of the manor, but leaving four daughters as co-heirs-Margaret wife of Richard Boteler, Isabel wife of John Leyburne, Mabel wife of Thomas Acclamby and Joan wife of Nicholas Acclamby. Each of them had a fourth part of the manor, but the descent is by no means clear, as the subdivisions are given differently at different times.

The Boteler share may be that held by the Butlers of Hackinsall. William Butler died in 1586 holding a fourth part of the manor of Hackinsall, with messuages and lands in Hackinsall, Preesall, Poulton, Thistleton, Staynall and Elswick. The heir was his grandson William, aged twenty-three, who died in 1613 holding a moiety of the manor of the king in socage, and leaving a son Henry to succeed him. Henry's daughter Ellen carried the estate to William Fyfe of Wedacre. Their daughter Catherine became heir, and marrying John Elletson, this part of the manor has descended to Mr. Henry Chandos Elletson of Parrox Hall. He is said to hold a third part of the manor.

Hackensall Hall in 2017

Parrox Hall is a low two-story H-shaped house with rough-cast and whitewashed walls and grey slated roofs, very much modernized, but still preserving some of its ancient features. The building itself offers no architectural evidence of a date earlier than the first half of the 17th century, but there have been so many alterations at different times that it is quite possible the structure may incorporate parts of an earlier building, though whether of date prior to the 16th century it is impossible to say. Any earlier building which may have stood on the same site was probably pulled down wholly or piecemeal at the time the present house was erected or came into being.

The principal front, which is about 75 ft. in length, is now north, but this is probably a later modification of the original design, the entrance having been most likely on the south side, now the garden front. The east or kitchen wing is over 60 ft. in length, but the west wing is very much shorter with only a slight projection north and south. The original plan appears to have been changed, perhaps more than once, and how far the modern work reproduces old features it is now impossible to say. An arched entrance at the south end of the east wing, if it represents in any way an older feature, suggests the entrance gateway to a courtyard on the south side of the house.

Knott End

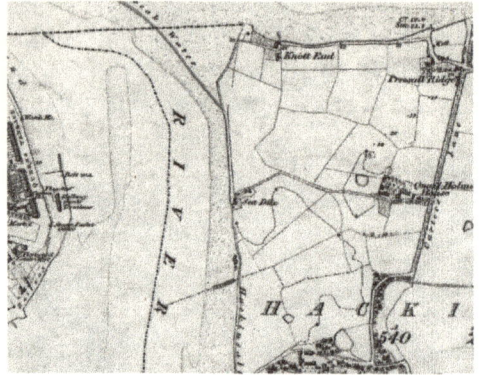

This is a 6in map of the area around Knott End in 1848. It forms part of the township of Preesall with Hackensall on the east bank of the River Wyre which rises in the Forest of Bowland. Hackensall and Knott have Norse roots. The 'knotts' were two large mounds of stones which lay out in the river until they were destroyed in the construction of Wyre Dock. The map shows very few buildings on it. Sea Dike cottage is on the river bank and there is a building which is possibly an alehouse which is near the shore. This alehouse is probably the forerunner of the Bourne Arms Hotel which was erected about 1850. On the 1851 census the population of the Preesall with Hackensall district was 823 with about 150 of these living in Knott End. The majority who were in occupation were connected with the sea and river such as fishing. By 1861 the population in the district had fallen to 821 with the majority engaged in maritime and farming activities. The first ferry services were operated by local fishermen who took passengers across the river on an informal basis. Following the commencement of work on Fleetwood new town there was a growth in the service and by 1851 fourteen small boats and a steam launch were in operation.

In the House of Lords meeting to discuss the Act for The G&KER Railway in June 1864 the chairman asked the witness Mr Henry Gardner, who owned considerable property in Pilling, "What is Knot End?" Mr Gardner replied "It is the promontory nearest Fleetwood. It joins the river Wyre, and is the only place at which a communication can be established between Fleetwood and the mainland. Agricultural produce was already carried across the Wyre at Knot End by means of ferry boat." The chairman (the Earl of Devon) asked, "is there a town at Knott End?" Mr Gardner answered "No, there is only a public house and some farm buildings. A few years ago Fleetwood was a fashionable bathing place, but since the North Euston Hotel was taken by the government and converted into a barracks all that has entirely changed. No family will go there now; but if this railway was made I believe it would be an inducement for them to go to Knot End."

*   *   *   *

Lancaster to Preston Railway

The Lancaster and Preston Junction Railway was an early British railway company which later merged with the Lancaster and Carlisle. It was created by an Act of Parliament on 5 May, 1837, obtained by a group of local merchants and entrepreneurs, to link Lancaster and Preston. The line was 20 miles long and was built by Joseph

Locke. In 1838 they were building the line, which was fairly level and straight, with few engineering problems. The biggest challenge was building the viaduct across the Conder valley at Galgate. It opened on 25 June, 1840 with a passenger service the next day. The station was built on the modern day South Road just south of the Lancaster Canal. The original station called Penny Street, now set among the buildings of the hospital, still survives.

Traffic was disappointing in the early stages due to the Lancaster Canal lowering its fares on its packet boats. The canal also went through the centre of Garstang whereas the railway station was a mile and a half from the centre.

The Lancaster and Preston Junction Railway faced increasing financial difficulties and with other railway companies showing no interest took the unusual step of leasing the line to the Lancaster Canal which was well managed and this arrangement continued for some time.

On the 21 August, 1848 a Euston to Glasgow express train ran into the back of a stationary train at the Bay Horse Station. One woman passenger was killed and a number of others injured with several of the carriages being wrecked. The subsequent enquiry laid part of the blame on the uncertainty over the ownership of the line. The canal company accepted compensation to relinquish the use of the line. The London and Carlisle Railway leased the line from 1 August, 1849. Soon after this The Lancaster and Preston Junction Railway joined forces with the Lancaster and Carlisle in 1859 and the L&CR was leased to and then amalgamated with the London and North Western Railway in 1879. It had had a short independent life of only 13 years.

Glasson Dock was connected to the rail network with a line to Lancaster in 1883, the line closed to passengers on 5 July, 1930 with goods traffic continuing until 7 September, 1964.

*   *   *   *

The Lancaster Canal.

The canals and the railways came about because of the need to transport goods easily. The roads and road transport were in such a terrible state that it was easier to import goods from overseas into ports. Lancaster was an important port in the 1700s but the shifting sands of the tidal Lune made it a difficult port to enter. Coal reached Lancaster and the surrounding district by sea from the River Douglas, so in an effort to save Lancaster a canal was proposed starting at Kendal and running south through Preston and onto the Leeds and Liverpool Canal. In 1771 at a meeting at Lancaster it was decided that a survey should be made. James Brindley was approached and he let his pupil, Robert Whitworth, do it. The scheme did not attract much support and an alternative port at Glasson was proposed.

In 1791 the scheme for a canal was revived and in October John Rennie, the engineer, was requested to make a survey. By early 1792 he had undertaken the survey and come up with a plan for a broad canal. It would start at Westhoughton, in the middle of the coalfields, then cross the Ribble to Preston by an aqueduct and northwards by Garstang and Ashton to Lancaster. It would cross the Lune and then to Kendal via Tewitfield. This received an enthusiastic welcome and an Act of Parliament was obtained. John Rennie was appointed engineer in July, 1792 and the contracts started to be awarded from December. The aqueduct over the Ribble was never built and the rest of the works were often delayed and disputed. The section, south of the Ribble, was sold to the Leeds and Liverpool Canal.

Broken Back Bridge Number 93. An early colour postcard of the Lancaster Canal

On November 22nd, 1797, the Lancaster Canal was formally opened from Preston to Tewitfield and after a long period of delays and lack of funds the section to Kendal was opened on June 18th, 1818. The Glasson Dock branch was opened in May, 1826. The tonnage carried on the canal almost doubled between 1820 and 1825. In 1829 the Ribble Navigation Company stated that Foreign trade vessels had left the port for the advantages of Glasson Dock. In 1830 sixty four ships had passed over the canal and by 1840 the number had risen to one hundred and eighty five ships. But shadows were being cast over Lancaster Canal and others by the arrival of the railways. In 1837 a Bill was put before Parliament for the construction of a railway between Preston and Lancaster and the canal company objected to the bill to no avail. The Lancaster and Preston Junction Railway opened in June, 1840 and a few weeks later the Preston and Wyre Railway opened to Fleetwood. The canal company halved their fares between Lancaster and Preston and continued to carry about the same number of passengers. The railway company got into difficulties and was leased by the canal company in 1842. The company was affected by the Lancaster and Carlisle Railway, which took trade from the Kendal stretch and also the Preston and Wyre Railway which took trade from Glasson as the docks at Fleetwood were expanding. The Lancaster Canal Company was formally dissolved in January, 1886, when the London and North Western Railway purchased the canal outright.

WYRE AQUEDUCT
A SINGLE SPAN AQUEDUCT, 110 FEET LONG, CARRYING THE CANAL 34 FEET ABOVE THE RIVER WYRE.
ENGINEER: JOHN RENNIE
FIRST USED 1797

As a memento a number of commemorative silver medallions were struck showing the Lune aqueduct. The London and North Western Railway managed the canal from Lancaster and in 1883 opened a branch line from Glasson Dock to Lancaster.

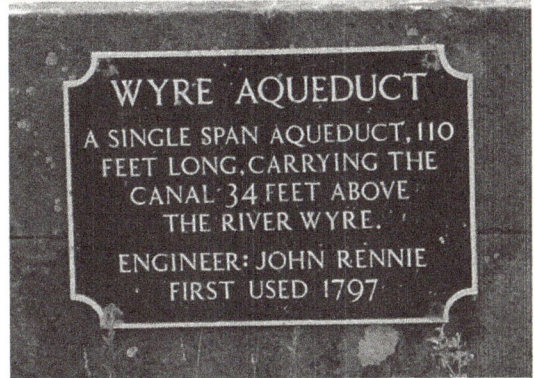

*   *   *   *

The maps are 6" to the mile 1914 Ordnance Survey maps and follow the route from west to east. The pictures are the track and building remains in 2017.

Line of track eastwards to Garstang

Cutting in Wildgoose Wood to main line

Taylor Bridge just north of where the main line is joined at Catterall

Nateby Crossing Cottage

Remains of the bridge over the canal looking from the west

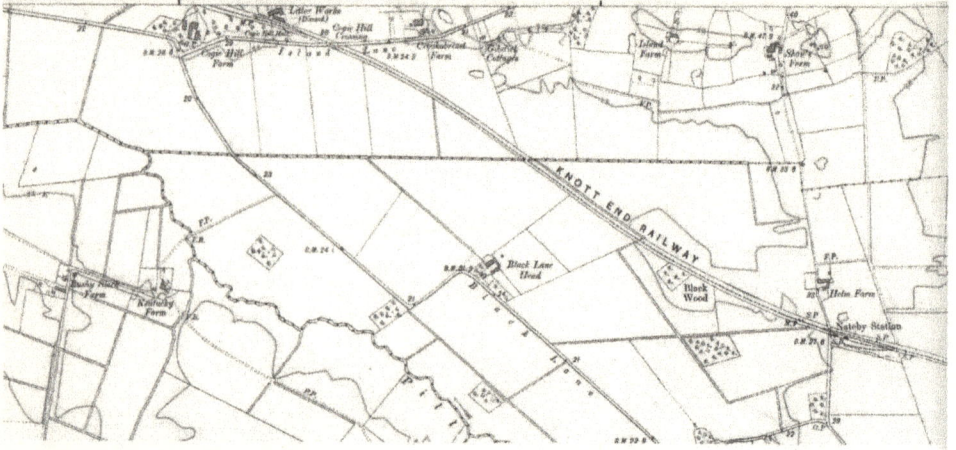

Track west from Nateby Station

Site of Nateby Station

Cogie Hill Cottage

Garstang Road Halt at Pilling

Pilling Station

Top is the railway barrow outside old station house.

This Hudswell Clarke 0-6-0ST restored and is at the entrance to the caravan site in Pilling.

Nicknamed the 'Pilling Pig.'

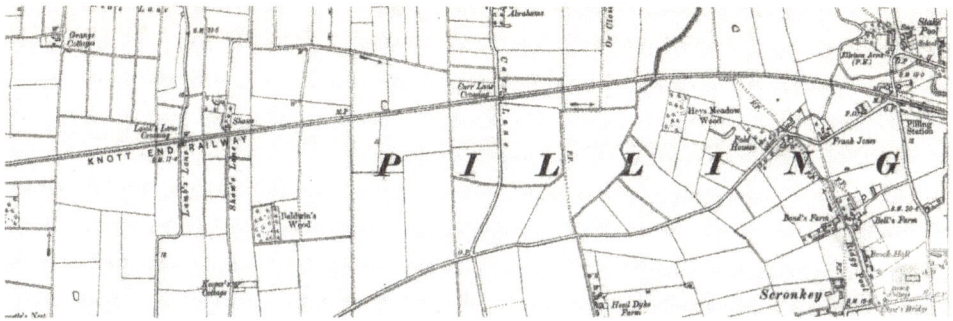

Carr Lane Crossing

Lamb's Lane Crossing

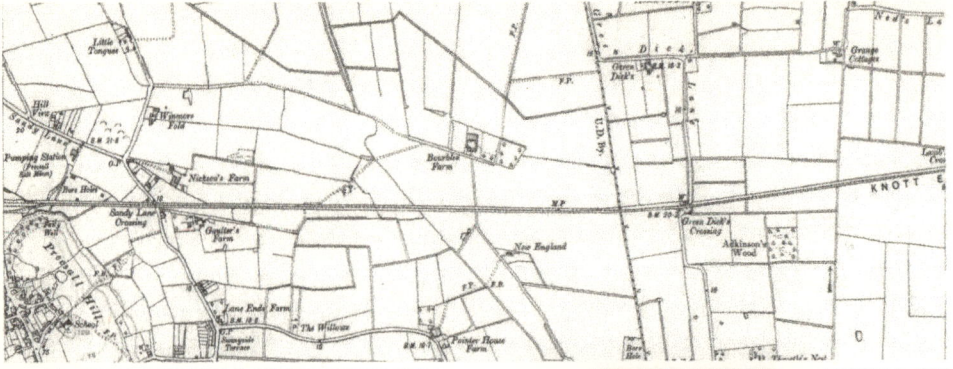

Green Dick's Crossing

Sandy Lane Crossing

Track looking east towards Preesall Bridge

Knott End Station

The Coming of the Railway

The northern portion of the Fylde was formerly known as Amounderness, though the name has now fallen into disuse and Fleetwood should be the place where the produce of Amounderness would pass through. Sir Peter Hesketh Fleetwood, who gave his name to the town, realised that the estuary of the Wyre could become a major port. The first house were erected in Fleetwood in 1836, with the first quays along the river arriving in 1840, and the port gradually expanding over the years. The Preston & Wyre Railway opened with a single line on 15 July 1840 with a doubling of the line between 1846 and 1851. Unfortunately Knott End immediately opposite Fleetwood is separated by about 400 metres of the Wyre estuary. This could not be easily bridged due to the amount of shipping using the channel. Shard Bridge was eventually built but this entailed a detour of approximately 13 miles. The farmers of the district looked to the east at Garstang for an outlet for their goods, but the roads were narrow and winding and progress to Garstang Market was slow and burdensome. Notable in the work of bringing the soil of the moss into cultivation was the Squire of Rawcliffe, Wilson ffrance. A main ditch was dug, traversing Rawcliffe Moss, Stalmine Moss and Pilling Moss, which reached the sea near Pilling where a sluice gate was built to prevent the sea flooding into the ditch. Land drains were then connected to the ditch from all parts of the area. It was Wilson ffrance who persuaded the local landowners to back a plan for a railway from Knott End to connect with the London & North Western Railway (then still the Lancaster & Preston Railway) at Garstang & Catterall station. Mr ffrance's agent, John Addie contacted a civil engineer by the name of James Tolme and arranged for him, at Easter, 1863, to lay out the course of a railway from Garstang to Knott End.

A meeting of landowners and other gentlemen was held at the Royal Oak Inn, Garstang on Thursday 12 November 1863 for the purpose of considering the desirability or otherwise of applying to parliament for powers to construct a railway. Given as one of the reasons for the railway was to afford better trading facilities to the farmers so they would endeavour to become more competitive and produce more, the soil would be better looked after and the land would necessarily become more fruitful. It was also pointed out that halfway between Preston and Lancaster there is a halting place on the railway, called "Garstang Station," but those who expect the town to which it refers in that locality will be woefully deceived. The fact is, the building now palmed off as "Garstang Station," is nowhere; it is near no place; and its location only aggravates honest people, who expect to be at the place they have booked for. The town of Garstang is two miles from the station which bears its name, and such a distance involves an uncomfortable and most unreasonable journey on the part of those who have business to transact or friends to see.

The route of the new railway will be as follows-after leaving Knott End, it will verge along south of Parrox Hall. Then it will turn slightly northwards, leaving Preesall (where there will be a station) to the right. A still more northern direction will then be pursued. The extreme point of divergence on that side being reached near Pilling. There will be a station here. This, it is probable, will have to serve for Stake Pool. After leaving the latter place on the left, the line will take its course past Crawley's Cross, and down to Cogie Hill. There will be another station here. The subsequent route will be in almost a straight line to Garstang. The entrance to Garstang will be on the northern side of the town, near the Independent Chapel. At Garstang there will, of course, be a station-the principal one. The line will then proceed directly, by junction, into the Lancaster and Preston Railway, at or near the present station. It is probable that, if the railway is formed, docks and a steam ferry will be made at Knott End. These will not only accommodate, but largely facilitate, passenger and goods traffic.

At the meeting Mr H Gardner occupied the chair. There was a numerous attendance, and amongst those present were Dr. Hall, of Fleetwood; Mr Tarner, Fleetwood; Mr Bennett, Liverpool; Mr Addie, Mr Paul Catterall, jun., Mr Allen and Mr R Gardner.

Mr Harlin (the representative of the engineer) gave the meeting some information relative to the new line and indicated that the cost of the line would not be very much, the gradients would be very favourable, and the entire sum needed would not be more than £60,000 which included the stations and included everything apart from the rolling stock. The estimate they had made would show a net profit of at least five per cent on the outlay of the line. He happened to be at Knott End the other day, and he there heard a farmer say that if the line was made he should keep one horse less than at present. That would amount to about £25 a year. He said they had taken the land at the rate of eight acres per mile. This would give them a mean width of 66 feet, amply sufficient to make a double line. He estimated everything at the market price, and he put down the land at £100 per acre. The land was very level, and in case of necessity he thought it would include sufficient to enable them to lay double rails. If they got too little in the first instance, the landowners would probably not like to be troubled with a second application for more. Mr Bennett asked how long the line, when commenced, would take in formation and Mr Harlin replied that he would say fifteen months would be ample. The motion to move forward with the proposals was carried.

From The Preston Chronicle 14 November, 1863.

Further meetings were held at Garstang and at Pilling on Friday 27 November, 1863. Garstang was held at the Town hall in the morning with Mr Taylor the bailiff in the chair and was described as a meeting of the inhabitants of Garstang and the neighbourhood to consider to what extent the proposed Garstang and Knot End Railway should be encouraged by them. The chairman after explaining the objects of the proposed railway and the intended route asked Mr Addie whether there was any intention of making docks on the Knott End side of the estuary. Mr Addie said he would say that no such thing was intended by the promoters or any one of the supporters of the projected railway. He would pledge his word and honour as a gentleman that if such a thing was in future attempted he would at once wipe his hands of the whole affair.

Mr Thornton raised a point at the meeting that he thought that if a station were placed at the Island Farm, Nateby, occupied by Mrs Balderson, instead of at Cogie Hill, it would be much better for the district, and for a very small outlay Pilling and Winmarleigh could be very greatly benefited. There was a small neck of land between Richard Singleton's and Helm Farm, and if a road were made through the neck of land, Winmarleigh would be connected with the Island, and the occupiers of land in the neighbourhood of Eagland Hill and Out Rawcliffe might be easily connected with the Island through Jackson's land. There are thirty five farms in that district, and if the station were made at Cogie Hill the people would bring their produce to Garstang by road, so that the traffic on the line would be lost. The station should be placed where he had named, if they intended the scheme to pay. Mr Thornton was told that this matter would be dealt with after the Bill had been passed in parliament. A motion that the meeting was favourable to the proposed scheme was passed.

A meeting was held on the Friday afternoon at the house of Mr W Bousfield, Stakepool Inn, Pilling which went through the same information and the motion was passed.

On the 12th December a letter was published in the Preston Herald saying that the proposed railway would spoil a plan to have two railways from Knott End, one passing through Pilling and Glasson to Lancaster, the other one passing through Stalmine, Great Eccleston and Inskip to Preston. (Glasson Dock was eventually joined to Lancaster by rail in 1883).

This letter also mention that the best plan, both for opening the district in question and promoting the establishment of a dock at Knott End was to forward a motion for forming two railways.

In the same paper was an advertisement offering 6,000 shares at £10 each in a mini prospectus.

In December 1863 a prospectus was printed for the "Garstang And Knot(t) End Railway" to raise share capital of £60,000 in 6,000 shares of ten pounds each.

"A deposit of 5s per share to be made on application, which will be returned less the actual disbursements in Parliament, should the application for the act prove unsuccessful during the present Session of Parliament".

The provisional committee members were-Colonel James Bourne, Heathfield House, Wavertree. Julian Augustus Tarner Esq., Queen's Terrace, Fleetwood. Richard Bennett Esq., Mulberry House, West Derby. Henry Gardner Esq., Barrister-at-Law, Sion Hill, Garstang. John Rossall Esq., Newton Hall, Clitheroe.

The engineers were W R Galbraith Esq. and Julian H Tolme Esq., 19 Duke Street, Westminster, London.

Solicitors Messieurs Hargrove Fowler & Blunt, 3 Victoria Street, Westminster, London, and Mr Paul Catterall, 6 Camden Place, Preston.

Secretary Mr John Addie, 18 Fox Street, Preston.

Bankers-The Lancaster Banking Company and Branches, and Messieurs Barclay, Bevan & Company, Lombard Street, London.

Prospectus in the Preston Chronicle 19 December 1863

Commencing at the Port of Fleetwood, this line will pass through "Preesall," "Pilling," "Cogie Hill," "Nateby," "Garstang," and join the London and North Western Railway, thus bringing the above neighbourhood into direct communication with the West Riding of Yorkshire, the Ports of "Hull," "Newcastle," etc, on the Eastern Coast and other important districts connected with the North Western system.

It is established in consequence of an urgent demand for railway accommodation in the district, and is brought forward on purely mercantile grounds, to supply a growing public want; in proof of which the farmers, landowners and residents along the whole line of the railway, are favourable to, and are taking shares in the undertaking.

The course of the line (ten and a half miles in length) is mostly level, and entirely free from engineering difficulties, the result being that it will be unusually cheap to construct.

The ancient Market Town of "Garstang" has hitherto been virtually without railway communication. It claims to possess the cheapest market in Lancashire for agricultural produce. The resources of the country on each side of the Railway are very large, and it is confidently anticipated that by extending to merchants, farmers, graziers and others, transit accommodation on a liberal scale, the traffic from the resources of the locality alone will pay nearly 5 per cent of the capital after allowing for working expenses.

Independently of local traffic, arising from agricultural produce, it is confidently expected that the receipts from imports of cattle, flax, provisions, machinery, etc., into the Wyre and the general interchange of commodities between Ireland and the great manufacturing districts, will yield an ample return on the proposed capital.

Professor Phillips, in his Mineral Reports of the District, declares the probability of coal occupying the centre, and, with this line in progress, and a cheap and speedy communication thereby afforded to the harbour of "Wyre," there is little doubt but the landowners will be prompted to develop the mineral wealth which may be found.

Passengers from Scotland, and tourists from the Lakes and North of England, on their way to the Military Schools and fashionable Marine Watering Towns of Fleetwood, Blackpool, and Lytham, would effect a saving of twenty miles by the use of this route.

The capital of the Company has been fixed at £60,000 with power to borrow om mortgage to the amount of one third of that sum, when half of the capital has been subscribed, and the Provisional Committee are satisfied by the plans and estimates submitted to them that the proposed capital of £60,000 will be amply sufficient to bring the undertaking to a successful issue.

Application is intended to be made to Parliament for an Act for the above mentioned Railway in the ensuing session, and if the Bill is obtained, the operations of the Company will be immediately commenced, and the Line, from its simple character, may be opened for traffic in twelve months after the commencement.

Forms of Application for shares may be obtained from the Secretary. Mr John Addie, Fox Street, Preston. The Brokers of the Line Mr William Welch, Lancaster, Mr John Rawlins Postlethwaite, Preston and Mr James Roper, 18 Dale Street, Liverpool.

Also at the Temporary Offices of the Company, 18 Fox Street, Preston.

The prospectus claimed that the proposed line would be the most direct connection between Fleetwood and the industrial areas of Lancashire and Yorkshire and would eventually link up to the Port of Hull. It also did not rule out the provision of a harbor at Knott End and this caused the Lancashire & Yorkshire and London & North Western Railways to object.

The House of Commons met on the 27th April 1864 and the House of Lords on the 14th June to decide on the bill. The following was reported in the press.

On Wednesday 27th April 1864 the committee on the Garstang & Knot End Railway bill met with Mr Adair in the Chair

Mr Rodwell, Q.C.. and Mr Garth, appeared for the promoters; and Mr Morreweather, Q.C.; Mr V Harcourt, Q.C.; and Mr S Pope, opposed for the London and North Western and Lancashire and Yorkshire Railway Companies.

Mr Garth opened the case by saying that the proposed line will pass through an agricultural district including Pilling, Preesall and Nateby. There are now large quantities of potatoes produced in the district, but there are parts not cultivated, and we say this railway would bring them into cultivation. He stated there would be no problem with the engineering side as the country is a flat one, the line will be easily made and consequently there will be no pecuniary difficulties. He also made the point that there are landowners who are willing to take payment for their land with shares. The bill projects three railways, one from Knot End to Garstang itself, or rather to the junction-that is ten miles and three furlongs; No. 2 is a small portion that runs up to the north; and No. 3 is a portion which would run down from the junction south to the Garstang station on the London and North Western line.

Mr John Addie, land agent for the promoters said he believed the owners, through whose land the railway passed, were favourable to the scheme. He had taken the quantities of the land and ninety one acres would be required. 28 owners had assented to the scheme, there were 6 neuters in number; dissentients were three and there were no answers from 19.

There was then further discussions about the amount of produce, potatoes, wheat and oats, and how these would be assisted by the building of the line, and then they adjourned for the day resuming on the Thursday with more evidence from landowners about the benefits the line would bring. Mr John Taylor said he was at present bailiff of

Garstang. The population at present was about 800; it had rather decreased than increased. The scheme proposed would be a great convenience. Garstang was the best market in North Lancashire, excepting Preston. The present station on the London and North Western line was 2 miles from Garstang and the road was a bad one. The road to the Bay Horse Station was a tolerably good one, but there was a turnpike to pass through. He had not heard a dissentient voice among the farmers as to the necessity of this railway. Mr Wolf, agent to Col. Wilson Patton, said the colonel owned the township of Winmarleigh. The proposed line would pass though two miles of his property. He did not know a district that stood more in need of a railway, and the one projected would be a great convenience. Mr Richard Robinson, agent to Mr Keppel, who owns the whole of Garstang, said Mr Keppel was strongly in favour of the line. It would be a great improvement and convenience to the district.

Mr Tolme, engineer of the project then gave evidence. "I went over the line as early as Easter, 1863, and in November, I went over it for the purpose of making the plans. The line is divided into three parts, No. 1 is 10 miles 3 furlongs and 6 chains, No. 2 is 37 chains long, and No.3 is 73 chains. The country is very level. The deepest cutting on line No. 1 will be 19 feet, and the highest bank 21 feet. The steepest gradient is 1 in 100; that is about three miles from the commencement of the line at Garstang." His estimate of the cost of construction was No1. £51,157, No.2 £2,821 and No. 3 £5,073, a total of £59,051. To Mr Pope he said this is a single line, but the arrangements are directed for a double line. My directions were to lay out a local line, and that is the reason why I adopted the level crossings. At three of the level crossings we propose stations, one of which is at Stakepool, near to Pilling, and one at Preesall. To the Chairman he said the moss land is quite capable of sustaining the permanent way. There are about five miles of moss, all under cultivation. The schedule of prices has been submitted to Mr Allen, the contractor. He agrees to take the contract for £3,000 less or about £57,000. I think the line can be constructed in twelve months.

Mr George Willoughby Hemans, engineer, said he had made a great many railways in Ireland. He had been over the projected line and made an examination. There was no difficulty in laying it out, and the design had, he thought, been well conceived. There was no inconvenience in these level crossings when properly treated. The moss presented no difficulties of construction. In a level country of this kind to build bridges over the roads would be an absurdity. The estimates were more than sufficient.

That concluded the evidence for the promoters and after a speech by Mr Pope the committee consulted and the Chairman then said they were of the opinion that the preamble of the bill had been satisfactorily proved.

House of Lords Tuesday 14 June 1864

The select committee appointed by the House of Lords in connection with The Garstang and Knot End Railway Bill met. The Earl of Devon was in the chair with the other members being Earl Cowpe, Lord Southampton, Lord Hatherton and Lord Leigh.

Mr Rodwell, Q.C.. and Mr Garth, appeared for the promoters of the bill and Mr Hope Scott Q.C., Mr Vernon Harcourt, and Mr Pope appeared for the opposition, the London and North Western and Lancashire and Yorkshire Railway Companies.

Much of the evidence was similar to the House of Commons meeting and Mr Rodwell said, it was a simple and unpretending line, proposed entirely for the accommodation of the local traffic of the district. It was originated by the landowners and inhabitants of the district, and up to this moment had received very considerable local support, both pecuniary and otherwise. It was alleged, by scientific men, that minerals existed in the district, but that was not an essential part of the present scheme. It was not at present proposed to construct a double line, and as the country was very flat, there would be no engineering difficulties to contend with.

Mr Henry Gardner, of Liverpool, who with his brother owned considerable property in Pilling. He said that the property there was almost entirely reclaimed, and was capable of great improvement. It was originally moss land. He had been present at all the public meetings in reference to the line, which were largely attended by the tenant farmers and by the representatives of the various landowners, who were unanimously in favour of the scheme. It was originally intended only to carry the line to Preesall. He did not know the reason why it had been carried to Knot End.

The Earl of Devon asked: "What is Knot End."

Mr Gardner: "It is the promontory nearest Fleetwood. It joins the river Wyre, and is the only place at which a communication can be established between Fleetwood and the mainland. Agricultural produce was already carried across the Wyre at Knot End by means of ferry boat."

The Earl of Devon: "Is there a town at Knot End."

Mr Gardner: "No, there is only a public house and some farm buildings. A few years ago Fleetwood was a fashionable bathing place, but since the North Euston Hotel was taken by the government and converted into a barracks all that has entirely changed. No family will go there now; but if this railway was made I believe it would be an inducement for them to go to Knot End. The sands are excellent, and the bathing is very good. The farmers in the locality will be greatly accommodated by the construction of this line."

After various evidence from farmers and landowners Mr Tolme C.E. stated that he had laid the line in Easter, 1863, at the request of Mr Addie, agent to Mr William ffrance, the present secretary of the line. The line consisted of three branches; one a main line from Garstang to Knot End, and two short branches, by means of which a junction would be effected with the Lancaster and Preston line. The total length of the main line was 10 miles 3 furlongs and 6 chains, the sharpest curve was three furlongs two and a half chains. The estimated cost of construction was £59,051.

The Earl of Devon asked: "Does that include stations?"

Mr Tolme: "Yes, and land also. There are to be stations at Garstang, Winmarleigh, Pilling, Preesall and Knot End."

Lord Leigh asked: "Is the land over which the line is to pass a bog?"

Mr Tolme: "No, it is moss, clay, and gravel. Originally it was peat, but most of it has now been brought into cultivation. There are no engineering difficulties to contend with.

That was the case for the promoters. The chairman said the committee were of the opinion that the preamble of the bill was proved.

The clauses were then agreed to, and the bill was ordered to be reported to the House.

The Bill received the Royal Assent on 30th June, 1864, with a five year limit for construction.

So the starting gate was reached with the difficult part out of the way. However it did not turn out that way. The directors and shareholders were quite naïve and the landowners and farmers soon began to go back on their stated intentions to sell the land at agricultural values and take payment in shares. They wanted cash for the land and impose conditions on which land to be used. The directors were very slow to exercise the powers that the act of Parliament gave them, but in the end the agreements with the farmers and landowners began slowly to come together.

At a meeting at the Royal Oak on the 22 August 1865 of the shareholders Mr H Gardner, the Chairman, said that an agreement had been made with Colonel Patten and Mr Bashall for the purchase of their land, and that Mr Keppel had given them immediate possession of his land; so that in the course of two or three days no doubt the work would be commenced.

At the same meeting Mr Addie submitted the following report;

"In January last the engineer of the company received an offer to construct the line from Mr John Bray, of Leeds, but the company's engineer, who had been deputed to confer with Mr Bray on the subject of the contract, was unable to agree with him as to the terms on which the undertaking was to be completed; that they now have the pleasure, however, to report that the construction of the line has been let to Mr Wheatley Kirk, of Manchester, for £82,000, which contract includes the value of the land wanted for the line, Parliamentary expenses, and all the expenditure of the makings of the line up to its completion. Mr Kirk is making active preparations to commence the works, possession of a portion of the land having been obtained, and negotiations with other landowners having been concluded; that in addition to shares agreed to be accepted by landowners in lieu of purchase money for land, a considerable number of shares have been applied for, and the deposit of 5 shillings per share has been paid; and your directors feel confident that as soon as the line has been commenced there will be a considerable addition to the number of shareholders."

> THE GARSTANG AND KNOT END RAILWAY.—The inhabitants of the Fylde district have now some prospect of being early benefitted by the Garstang and Knot End Railway. The contracts for the formation of the line have been let to Mr. Kirk, of Manchester, and the work is to be proceeded with immediately.

Preston Chronicle 5th August 1865

The chairman, Mr Gardner, then came up with an extraordinary idea which typified their grandiose thoughts at the time; he said

"The company had been put into a remarkably good position. Since they obtained power to make their line, application had been made to make a line from Bradford to

Colne, which was in a direct line with Knot End and Garstang, and almost in a direct line with the port of Hull. If that Act were passed and the line made, there would only be 20 miles of rails wanted to get a direct communication between Fleetwood and Hull, and the whole of Yorkshire. It was the opinion of many that with the facilities to commerce afforded by railways going through a large and populous county, that line would become a very important one in that part of the country. At present, to get into Yorkshire from Fleetwood they were obliged to go to Lancaster, and from Lancaster round by Skipton. He believed there was in the neighbourhood of Burnley some of the largest cattle fairs in the country, and there would be through communication for the cattle landed at Fleetwood or Knot End from Ireland. These cattle might easily be taken into Yorkshire, or, if it were needed, to the port of Hull, and there re-shipped. If the Act were passed for making the line between Bradford and Colne, he thought that very shortly afterwards the 20 miles link would be added, and their little local line would be an acting line with one of the greatest lines in the country-that of the Great Northern."

It did not seem to bother them that the hills of Bowland were in the way of a line to Colne. They were also optimistic of docks being built at Knott End.

The progress of the work was haphazard as the contractors were starting work on land that had not yet been bought and paid for. This was typified by a letter that John Addie, the secretary of the company sent to P Gregson Esq., Canal Office, Lancaster on the 13th September

"Dear Sir

I went to Garstang and Nateby yesterday and found the contractors manager had stopped the works on Nateby Hall Farm, but had commenced cutting on the Swarbrick land and had put a little soil on land in the occupation of Mr Wilding, which work I also stopped at once. The contractor's manager had commenced the work on both portions of your property purely by mistake. I hope it will be convenient for you to see me tomorrow in reference to the price of the land."

The press were still reporting optimistic reports of the progress.

THE GARSTANG AND KNOT END RAILWAY.—The workmen engaged on the new railway which is to connect Garstang with Knot End are making great progress. The route for the line of rails has been staked, and that part which passes the railway on the outskirts of Garstang has been cut; and the bridge over the road is in a very forward state. The railway is expected to be opened for traffic towards the close of next year.

Preston Herald 4th November 1865

A month later, at the beginning of December another report appeared in the Preston Chronicle stating that the new line of railway was progressing rapidly and that the route from Nateby to near Preesall (they probably meant Pilling) was ready for ballasting. A bridge at Garstang was nearly ready with the exception of the fixing of iron girders. A note of caution was creeping in though with the last line saying that the idea of extending the line to Clitheroe was being abandoned for the present.

At the next meeting of the shareholders at the Royal Oak Inn, Garstang, in February 1866 the engineer's report was read out. Significantly this was signed by Arthur S Hamond on behalf of Mr Tolme. It stated:

"The works on the line were commenced in the beginning of September last, since which time I have the pleasure of stating that the contractor has made satisfactory progress. The greater portion of the land is in the possession of the company, and a portion of it has been fenced off. About forty thousand cubic yards of earth have been removed in embankments, and about six miles of the line are ready for laying the ballast and permanent way. Arrangements are being made with the London and North Western Railway Company as to our junction with their line; as soon as they are completed the works at the east end of the line will be vigorously proceeded with. The weather, during the past two months, has prevented much work being done; but the contractor will, as soon as the season permits, proceed with the works so as to get them finished by the latter end of the ensuing summer."

The meeting also decided that an inspector of the line should be appointed, who was named as Mr Barnes, and he needed to ensure that good and efficient sleepers were used in its construction. Another of the shareholders said the sleepers which had already been used had been sanctioned and passed as good by the engineer. It appears even at this stage they were using secondhand materials.

Next under discussion was whether the station should be positioned at Cogie Hill or near Nateby. The chairman (Mr Gardner) thought that if there had to be a station erected at Nateby the landowners and farmers of the district should make the approach roads, as they would entail considerable expense and they could not expect Mr Kirk (the contractor) to make these approaches. Mr Taylor and Mr Noble had approached the farmers and landowners who had said they would provide a horse and cart to assist in making the approach roads and it was decided to place the station at Nateby.

Things started to go downhill from this point. In the Preston Chronicle 19th May 1866 it was reported *"That the works of this railway are again stopped, and it is not known when they will be resumed. On Monday last all the workmen received their wages, but have not been to work since. It is thought by many in Garstang that there has been a split amongst the principle officials, as one or two gentlemen have withdrawn from the offices they held."*

At the next meeting of the shareholders held at the end of August the secretary Mr Addie had resigned and been by replaced by Mr John Noble. The report from the engineer was read by the secretary.

"During the past six months, I regret to say that owing to the exceptional state of the money market, and various other causes, very little progress has been made with the works on your line. The greater portion of the land required for the railway is in possession of the company, and the rest can easily be obtained when required. The bridge over the turnpike road at Garstang is nearly completed, and the foundations of one abutment of the bridge over the river Wyre have been put in. All the culverts, with one or two exceptions, have been completed."

The directors also reported: "Since the last ordinary meeting of the company the works of the line have been suspended by the failure of the contractor, owing to severe pressure of the money market: but negotiations are now pending which, we trust, will enable the directors before long to resume operations; at the same time, we do not think it advisable to press the completion of the works until the rate of interest, is still further reduced."

So Mr Kirk, the contractor, had resigned his contract and handed it to the directors who, at this time, were not to keen to resume the works as the cost of money was so high and they were placed in a similar situation to nine-tenths of the railways in England and Wales, caused by the failures of their largest contractors, which had spread ruin. Mr Kirk, when he was about to become bankrupt had first transferred his contract to Mr Charles Reeves (his son-in-law) and then to Mr Hamond. It was at this meeting that the extension of the act of parliament to ask for more time to complete the works was discussed. It was expected to cost between £300 and £400. In November an advert was placed in the press to apply for extending the time for the completion of the works. This was for the 1867 Session.

Notice.

IN PARLIAMENT:—Session 1867.
GARSTANG AND KNOT END RAILWAY.
Extension of time for completion of works and purchasing lands, Amendment of act.

NOTICE IS HEREBY GIVEN, that application is intended to be made to parliament in the ensuing session by the Garstang and Knot End Railway Company for an act to extend the time granted by the "Garstang and Knot End Railway Act, 1864," for the completion of the works and purchase of lands by that act authorized, and to repeal or amend such act or the acts incorporated therewith, so far as may be necessary for such purpose.

Printed copies of the intended act will, on or before the 22nd day of December next, be deposited in the Private Bill Office of the House of Commons.

Dated this 7th day of November, 1866.

HARGROVE, FOWLER, and BLUNT,
3, Victoria-street, Westminster; and
PAUL CATTERALL,
6, Camden Place, Preston, Solicitors.
GREGORY, ROWCLIFFES, & RAWLE,
8, Parliament-street, Westminster,
Parliamentary Agents.

Preston Chronicle 17 November 1866

By December the contract for the works had been transferred to Allen & Co. Two directors Mr Noble and Mr Addie had resigned and joined Mr Allen to carry on building the line. At the February 1867 shareholders meeting, the directors congratulated the shareholders on having obtained such satisfactory contractors but put another dampener on the project by reporting little chance of any progress. The contractors had been paid with shares rather than cash and owing to continued difficulties in the financial world, they had been prevented from realizing the shares and thereby obtaining the necessary funds. The engineer reported:

"Very little progress has been made with the works. This, however, is owing to circumstance over which the contractors have no control, and is as unsatisfactory to them as to yourselves. The time has been principally occupied with negotiations for land purchase, and the completion of existing arrangements; also in getting materials on to the ground, in preparation for increased exertions when the weather is more settled. It is intended first to complete the line from Garstang to the junction, in accordance with your directions, and our principal efforts have been to obtain possession of the land from the river Wyre to the junction, which as yet we have not succeeded in doing."

So after all this time they were still struggling to obtain the land required to carry on with the works. The next meeting in August was titled in the newspaper "Uproarious Meeting." The shareholders and directors spent much of the meeting arguing about shares and who had paid what.. At this meeting the accounts were read by the secretary and deemed not worthy of publication. An interesting fact did emerge that since the last meeting £1,900 had been spent on the purchase of land, and that all the necessary land for the line had been purchased, with the exception of four plots. A total of £38,000 had been spent on contracting.

1868 started no better, in fact the situation deteriorated even more. The meeting held in February, at the Royal Oak Inn, had a bitter tone. The auditors' report was to the effect that there had been neither receipts nor payments since the last meeting. Mr Hammond (previously spelt with one N), who represented the engineer said that no work had been done on the line in the last six months, and therefore no money had been spent.

On the 12th March a special meeting of the shareholders was held "To take into consideration the steps to be taken for the purpose of urging upon the directors the necessity of prosecuting the works more vigorously." Mr John Noble and Mr Addie , who represented the contractors along with a few others put to the meeting that the main cause of the delay was that sufficient shares had not been subscribed for to enable the directors to proceed with the works as originally contemplated, and probably the directors would feel it necessary to ask the shareholders to sanction the substitution of a three foot gauge instead of the four feet eight and a half inches originally fixed upon. The idea being that when the conditions improved from the depression in the railway property the gauge could be returned to the larger size. Mr Addie was strongly in favour of the narrow gauge and he said " It was better, he thought, situated as they were, to take half a loaf than no bread for the present, and leave it time to bring everything they wanted. Meantime, the narrow gauge principle would undoubtedly pay the shareholders very well; and that, he thought, was far better than heedlessly scattering the shareholders' property to the winds." This did not go down very well and a resolution were adopted to form a defense association, with the view of urging the directors to proceed with the line.

Another meeting was held the following week to which reporters were not admitted but it was ascertained that the shareholders resolved to make a call of one shilling per share upon each member of the association. It was also agreed to engage Mr C T Clarke, solicitor, of Lancaster, to examine the railway contract and generally to advise as to the powers of the shareholders to compel the contractors to fulfil the contract.

The whole town, by this time was becoming very tired of the ongoing saga and the following letter appeared in the local press.

> **GARSTANG AND KNOTT END RAILWAY.**
> TO THE EDITOR OF THE PRESTON CHRONICLE.
>
> SIR,—I am waiting anxiously to see something turn up as to our railway, and I fully expected that before this time we should have had a good meeting of the inhabitants to take the concern into consideration. But what is everybody's business, seems to be nobody's. Will nobody in the town give the managers of this comparatively defunct scheme a "rub?" As an inhabitant I have always been an advocate of a better style of communication between Garstang and the Lancaster and Carlisle Railway, and I do not see why the portion of the new line intended to run between the town and railway named should not be gone on with. Surely if we can't have the whole, we may have a portion of the line made. I care little for an early resumption of the works in the direction of Knott End; my opinion is that that part of the line will never pay; but I do think that something might be made out of a railway between Garstang and the Lancaster and Carlisle line; and if carriages or trucks were only drawn by horses, we could put up with them until prospects became brighter. What are the directors waiting for? Is there more land difficulty?—more money difficulty?—or what? Perhaps they are waiting for a bid from the London and North Western Railway Co. Hoping that somebody will push up this poor affair—this miserable abortion of a railway,—I am yours, obediently,   A GARSTANG SHOPKEEPER.

Preston Chronicle 6th June 1868

By the next meeting in September this matter seems to have been resolved and the mood of the shareholders was impatient. They wanted to know when the contractors would carry on and finish the line. The company solicitor, Mr Catterall said that they could take it for granted that the contract would be in progress within four weeks. And their intention was to push the contractors to make the railway. It was stated by a representative of the shareholders that the time allowed for its construction would expire in June 1869, and unless some progress was made with the contract it could not be finished in time. Promises had been held out long enough; what they now wanted was performance.

This meeting also revealed that Mr Allen, the contractor, wished to be relieved from the contract and was not willing to take any further part in the making of the line. He had agreed to take a certain number of shares, and to pay cash (£4,000) for them. The cash was to be lodged in a joint account with directors and used to pay the contractors as the work proceeded. The other contractors were prepared to complete the contract on these conditions and had advertised and accepted the tender of a sub-contractor. Mr Addie said that the sub-contract would be agreed within two weeks and the works would be in progress within a month. The shareholders wanted to pursue the matter against Mr Allen but the solicitor, Mr Catterall, said that the state of Mr Allen's health made him deem it advisable to decline proceeding with the contract, and that the arrangement the directors had made with respect to the £4,000 was as favourable as they could effect after prolonged negotiation. The sub-contract was let to Mr Bush from Ulverston apparently a man of considerable experience. Even so an advert was placed in the newspapers in November to apply to parliament to extend the time for compulsory purchase of lands, completion of works and to increase the capital of the company. This was scheduled for parliamentary approval in 1869.

The next meeting in February 1869 was a little more optimistic. There was a fly in the ointment. The London and North Western Railway had been expected to move their station at Garstang closer to Turners Bridge which they had agreed to do, but as the railway had been so long a time in being resumed, they held themselves resolved from carrying out the agreement, therefore an increase in capital was needed for the making of a line known as No. 3 to meet up with the main line further south near to the existing station. The report from the engineer was read. This was still signed by J H Tolme but the Resident Engineer was Mr Hammond. The report read:

"I have much pleasure in reporting that during the past half year, satisfactory progress has been made with the works on this line, between Pilling and the junction with the London and North Western Railway. All the land required for the line has been purchased, and possession of it given to the contractors, with the exception of about half an acre near Garstang, and of some additional land which is required, upon which the line will be constructed from Turner's Bridge up to Garstang Station. All the bridges are complete, with the exception of that over the canal, and an occupation bridge, which cannot be built until the cutting near the North Western Line has been excavated. Should our operations not be delayed by any unforeseen cause, I have great hope that your railway will be opened as far as Pilling early in the summer."

The parliamentary act was passed and the extension to the time allowed.

"On the 3rd September 1869 several of the directors and their friends, and officers of the Garstang & KER, made an inspection of the line from Garstang to Stakepool. They were met at the Garstang Station by Mr Bush, the contractor, who conducted them to the proposed junction of the new line with the old. Near the junction bricks were being made for the erection of the bridges and stations which will be required in the immediate vicinity, and after inspecting these works the party mounted a wagon that had been prepared by Mr Bush for the occasion, and which was drawn by a horse. The line was then gone over as far as Stakepool. The number 1 cutting, which is rather expensive, was specially noticed, and also the bridge spanning the river Wyre. The bridge has iron girders, and a span of 64 feet, and is mainly constructed of bricks, as are most of the other bridges on the line. The clay used in the making of the bricks has been obtained from the cuttings in the making of the line. The bridge crossing the canal, which has a span of 74 feet, and is the most expensive structure of the kind in the whole length of the line, came in for special notice, and was declared to be satisfactory. The

bridge has been neatly and substantially constructed, and is in every way suitable for the purpose designed. The sites of the station and gate houses, and those buildings that have already been erected, were also inspected, and the party continued their investigations until they arrived at Cogie Hill, where they remained a short time, and thence proceeded on to near Stakepool, where most of the permanent way is weighed and ballasted. Only a small portion remains to be completed to finish the line up to Stakepool. The principal labour yet required to complete the line will be near the Garstang junction, for here four bridges will have to be erected, and some additional cutting done. The line is a single one, and for the greater part of the route the sleepers are laid longitudinally. Much cutting has been required between Garstang and Stakepool, but between the latter place and Knot End-the terminal of the line-little or no cutting will be needed. At Helm Farm, the party were met with conveyances, and were then conveyed back to Garstang, when they dined together at the Royal Oak Inn."

Subsequently the half yearly meeting of the share holders was held where the directors reported that the Act Of Parliament sanctioning the increase in capital and the extension of time for completing the line had received the royal assent. They also had under consideration the subject of providing the line with plant and rolling stock. The engineer's report was upbeat and declared that such progress had been made that it was almost ready for the visit of the Government Inspector. It was thought premature to go on with the whole of the line at once and it would be better to open the line as far as Stakepool before completing the line to Knot End.

A postcard of Stakepool at Pilling. This view is looking up Lancaster Road from the site of the station towards the Elletson Arms which was previously called the Gardner's Arms. The sign post is pointing right to Garstang.

The engineer's report at the next started in the usual way:

"During the past six months, such progress has not been made as was hoped for in my last report to you in the works remaining to be executed on this line, partly owing to our not having been able to obtain possession of the land belonging to The London and North Western Railway Company until about three weeks since, and partly to other causes beyond control. This is not so much, however, to be regretted, because the embankment over the moss, at Nateby, showed signs of weakness, which time alone should cure. It is now getting well consolidated, and fit for the passage of trains. The works remaining to be done on the main line will not, I hope, occupy many weeks. The stations have been proceeded with; that at Garstang will soon be finished. After the many delays which have taken place in the construction of the line, owing to financial difficulties and other causes, it is satisfactory to find that there is at least every apparent prospect of its speedy completion, and opening to the public."

The chairman summing up the meeting said "We are glad to see at least a fair prospect of the early completion, the advantages of which to the district will ultimately be of incalculable benefit, the locality comprising, as it does, a large part of the most productive land in the county, hitherto practically inaccessible, but which will be opened out by the new line now in formation; thus the new line joins the London and North Western line at Garstang and will, eventually, no doubt be extended eastward, to Skipton and that quarter, thus giving the Midland Counties direct access to Fleetwood and the ports on the north coast of Ireland." So even though they had taken so many years to build about seven miles of railway, they still had delusions of extending eastwards.

Progress was, however being made. A locomotive was ordered from Black, Hawthorn & Company. This was a 0-4-2 saddle tank named Hebe. Also four carriages were ordered from the Metropolitan Carriage Company, of Birmingham.

On Saturday the 11th June the first engine passed from the Preston and Lancaster Line to the Garstang and Knot End line where it made several journeys to Stakepool and back. It carried goods on some of the trips and did the same on the following Monday and Tuesday. The engine was hired from the London and North Western Railway. Towards the end of August the Government Inspector, Captain Tyler, together with Mr Bush, the contractor and Mr Hammond, the engineer and several others, passed over the line with two large and powerful engines and two carriages, in order to test the workmanship. The inspection went well and apart from a few minor alterations to the fencing and other small details which would be fixed within the week.

At the shareholders' meeting held at the end of August, the engineer said that the works were so far advanced that he was able to give notice to the Board of Trade of their intention to open the line for public traffic. He also said, optimistically, that preparations had been made for the completion of the remaining four miles to Knot End. The accounts showed that the amount expended up to the 30th June, 1870 was £105,410. 13shillings and that £12,231 was required to complete the undertaking. On the 26th October Captain Tyler, the Government Inspector, together with several members of the railway company, again inspected the line and passed it fit for opening.

The company did not have enough money to pay for the carriages that had been ordered and a company was formed on the 12th October, 1870. The following advert was in the Lancaster Gazette on the 29th October.

> GARSTANG ROLLING STOCK, LIMITED.—This is but a small company, a capital of but £5,000 in £5 shares being required. The particular object for which the undertaking has been launched is to provide the Garstang and Knot End Railway with rolling stock, &c. Undertakings of a similar character, on a larger scale, have been amongst the most successful of joint stock companies, and there is every reason to apprehend a like success for this enterprise, which may in course of time, as trade and commerce improve, extend both its capital and its sphere of operations.—"Railway News." Mr. Samuel Thompson, of Lancaster, is the chairman of this enterprise.

The wagon for the conveyance of goods arrived at the end of October and the four carriages a little later after a mishap. The usual train for Lancaster, which left at 9.10 with its own carriages and the four new ones for the Garstang and Knot End Railway. When the train set off and was going round the curve at the entrance to the tunnel the four new carriages ran off the line. They were got back on the line and another start made but they again came off the line blocking it. It was midnight before they finally made a successful start.

Hebe, the engine had been delivered without payment and was put to work by the company while deciding how to pay for it.

The line was finally opened on the 5th December, 1870 and the following report appeared in the Preston Chronicle on the 10th December.

"This new line of railway was opened on Monday for passenger traffic as far as Stakepool, a distance of about seven and a half miles. The line is opened from the London and North Western Railway by a junction, so that what formerly was called Garstang Station will now be known as Garstang Junction. The line is completed as far as Stakepool and the remaining portion-from Stakepool to Knott End-a distance of almost four and a half, will shortly be completed. The first cutting is through a red sandstone rock, close to Greenhalgh Castle. The line then runs between a deep enbankment as far as the River Wyre, over which is a bridge made of wrought iron girders, 64 feet span. Over the bridge the line is run on an embankment as far as Garstang Station, and for a short distance past this station the ground rises. The next bridge is over the canal, and is one of very substantial character. It is built of wrought iron girders, and is 74 feet span. At Nateby there is a cutting through a bed of clay, from which point the line runs through a deep enbankment on the moss to Winmarleigh. From that place the line runs pretty level to Stakepool, there being only one or two shallow cuttings between the two stations. The engine and carriages are built on the American principle, and the passengers pronounce them to be particularly comfortable.

The carriages are of two classes-first and third, and will each accommodate 52 passengers. The line is composed of longitudinal timbers and bridge rails, bolted down with fang bolts. There are cross transoms and bolts every 11 feet, the same as is now on the Great Western Line, where very powerful and heavy engines are working. The traffic since the opening of the line has been exceedingly great, indeed, more than really could be done. The line passes through a very productive portion of the Fylde, and is a great boon to the farmers of the district. They can now send their produce to almost any market, whereas prior to the line being opened, they had to have their produce carted to the various markets in the neighbourhood, or take it to Garstang Station, a distance of several miles. The line will also be very convenient for persons residing in the Fylde district travelling North. Instead of first booking to Preston, they can go by the new line to Garstang Junction, at a far less cost. Mr Bush, of Preston, is the contractor. The traffic has so increased that the company finds the waggons they now have are inadequate to their wants, and on Thursday a meeting of the Rolling Stock Committee took place in the Royal Oak Inn, Garstang, when it was decided to send out prospectuses for the purpose of obtaining contracts for new waggons. The inauguration dinner will take place on Wednesday, at the Royal Oak Inn, Garstang."

The formal opening of the Railway was celebrated at Garstang on the 14th December. A banquet was provided at the Royal Oak Inn. In the report in the Lancaster Gazette of 17th December a few interest points were noted of the people and the line.

"In the autumn of 1868 Messrs Noble and Addie, who may be fairly considered the financial contractors, sub-let a contract for the first section to Mr George Bush, a gentleman of some thirty years experience in railway contracts, and who has given proof in this instance of his capabilities to bring a contract to a creditable and successful issue. The railway and works have been designed and carried out under the superintendence of Mr A S Hammond C.E., of Birmingham, who has also designed the locomotive and the carriages which are of a novel kind being a something after the American idea, the object being economy in the working expenses; one guard having to book all the passengers in the train as the journey is made.

Between Pilling and Knot End the land is purchased for the line and some of it fenced in. The formation and culverts on most of the lengths are finished, and as there is only one bridge to build at Preesall and four and a half miles of road laying and ballasting to do, no doubt the company will soon complete the remainder of their railway. At Knot End it is in contemplation to construct docks and a steam ferry across the River Wyre, and if this is done no doubt can be entertained of the line eventually paying high dividends."

The Scorton band accompanied the train along the line to Stakepool. On their arrival at Stakepool, visitors were invited to refreshment provided in the Gardner's Arms. After luncheon the return journey was made to Garstang with the band meeting the train from Preston, which brought a further influx of visitors who all proceeded to the Royal Oak Inn to celebrate the inaugural proceedings.

*   *   *   *

GARSTANG AND KNOT-END RAILWAY

TIME TABLE for _____, 1870, and until further Notice.

NOTICE.

The published Time Tables of this Company are only intended to fix the time up to which Passengers may be certain to obtain their Tickets, for a journey from the various Stations, it being understood the Trains will not start before the appointed time. Greenwich time will be kept. Every effort will be made to ensure punctuality, as far as practicable, but the Directors give distinct Notice, that the Company will not undertake that the Trains shall start or arrive at the exact time specified in the Bills, nor will they be accountable for any loss, inconvenience, or injury, which may arise from delays or detention in the starting, transit, or arrival of Trains. Passengers can only be conveyed from intermediate Stations when there is room in the Train.

UP

Miles		1 a.m.	2 a.m.	3 No.3 a.m.	4 p.m.	5 p.m.	6 p.m.	7 p.m.	8 p.m.	9 p.m.
0	Pilling ... Leave	2 10	...	10 27	...	...	4 0	...	...	...
3	Winmarleigh ,,	7 26	...	10 37	...	4 12	...	...	...	...
5	Garstang ,,	7 38	10 35	10 45	7 0 2 25	4 22 5 17	8 25 9 20			
7	Garstang Junction Arrive	7 45	10 40	10 50	7 7 2 32	4 45 5 32	8 41 9 34			
	Do. (L.&N.W.) Depart	7 45	8 4	10 50	1 12 2 40	4 45 5 32	8 41 9 34			
	Preston Arrive	8 13	9 20	11 23	...	0 5 5 0	...			
	Lancaster ,,	8 55	...	11 25	1 48	... 5 20	6 53 10 5			

N.B. No.3, on Thursday, this Train will leave Pilling at 9 40, and Winmarleigh at 9 50, arriving at Garstang at ten o'clock, in time for the Market.

Nos. 1 and 16. These Trains will not run between Pilling and Garstang Town, except on Thursdays and Saturdays.

☞ All the Trains will take up and set down Passengers at Cockerham Cross and Cogie Hill Crossing, when required.

DOWN

Miles		10 a.m.	11 a.m.	12 a.m.	13 p.m.	14 p.m.	15 p.m.	16 p.m.	17 p.m.	18 p.m.
	Lancaster ... Leave	...	8 5	10 35	12 45	2 10	...	3 5	6 5	9 10
	Preston ,,	7 55	8 3	9 4	1 12	2 40	4 20	6 45	8 41	9 34
	Garstang Junction(L.&N.W.) Arrive	8 30	9 4	10 34	1 20	2 40	4 55	6 45	8 41	9 34
0	Garstang Junction Departs	3 50	10 11	11 0	1 20	2 45	5 0	6 55	50 0	40
2	Garstang ,,	...	9 20	11 7	1 22	2 52	5 7	6 42	50 0	46
4	Winmarleigh ,,	...	...	9 24	...	3 0	...	6 50	...	...
7	Pilling Arrive	...	...	9 30	...	3 10	...	7 0	...	...

All Trains First Class and Parliamentary.   No Sunday Trains.

PASSENGERS' LUGGAGE.—Every Passenger travelling upon this Railway may take with him his ordinary Luggage, not exceeding 120 lbs. if a first class passenger, and 60 lbs. if a third class passenger. Notice is however hereby given, that the Company will not be responsible for the care of the same, unless fully and properly addressed, with the name and destination of the party, nor for any article conveyed inside the carriage.

CHILDREN under three years of age, free; those above three, and under twelve, half-price.

By Order.

Offices, Garstang, Lancashire.

Wrightson, Printer and Stationer, Post Office, Garstang.

This is the first timetable of the new line. This was run by only one locomotive, "Hebe" It pulled a mixture if carriages and goods wagons for six days a week. Only Sunday was available for maintenance. The carriages were a mixture of first class and what the railway called "parliamentary" class.

Garstang Town Station. A painting from an old postcard

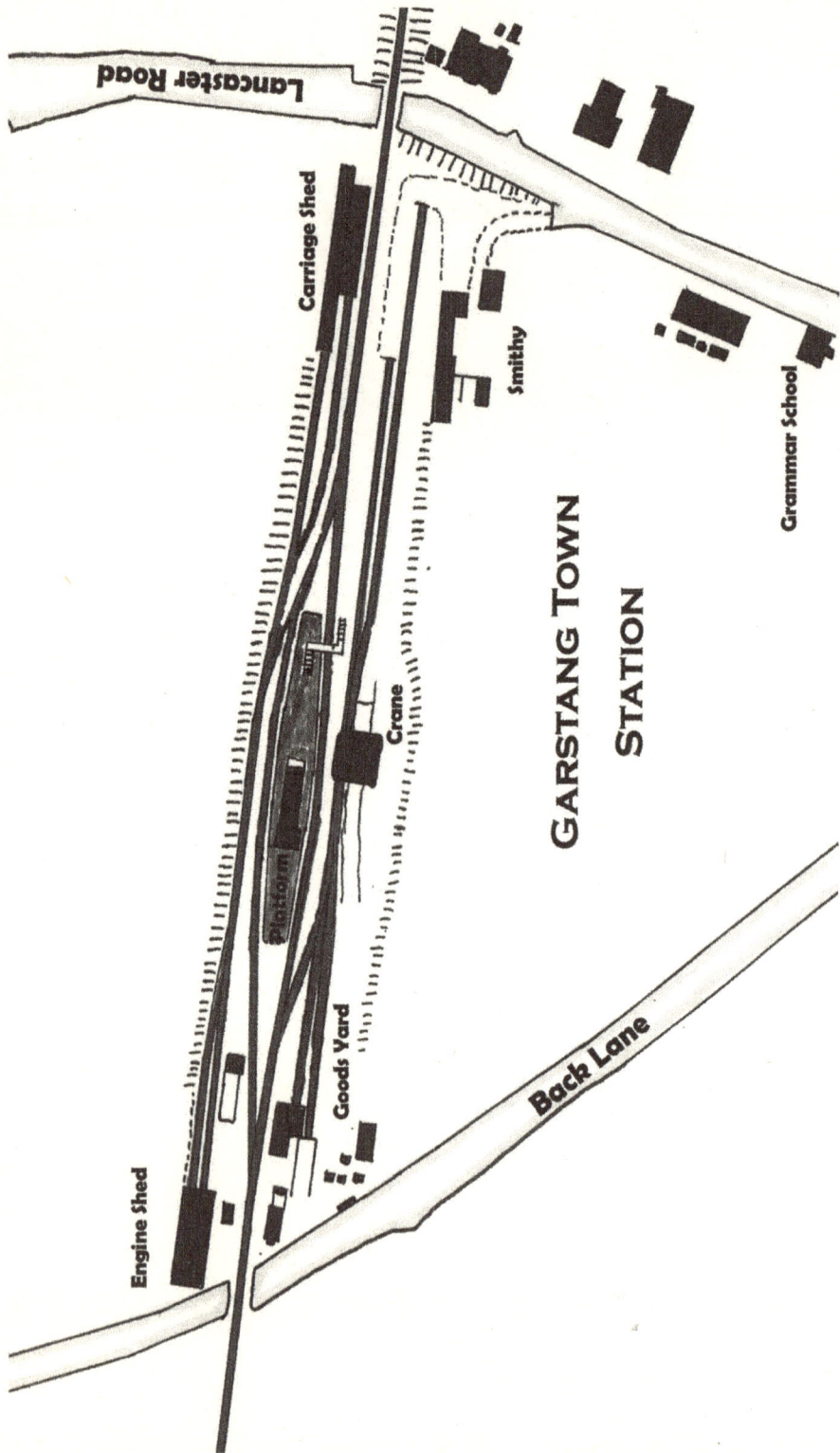

Garstang Town Station. A plan drawn from an early 20th Century Ordnance Survey Map

The following labels appear on the map:

Lancaster Road

Carriage Shed

Smithy

Grammar School

Engine Shed

Goods Yard

Platform

Crane

Back Lane

GARSTANG TOWN
STATION

Nateby Station. A painting from an old postcard

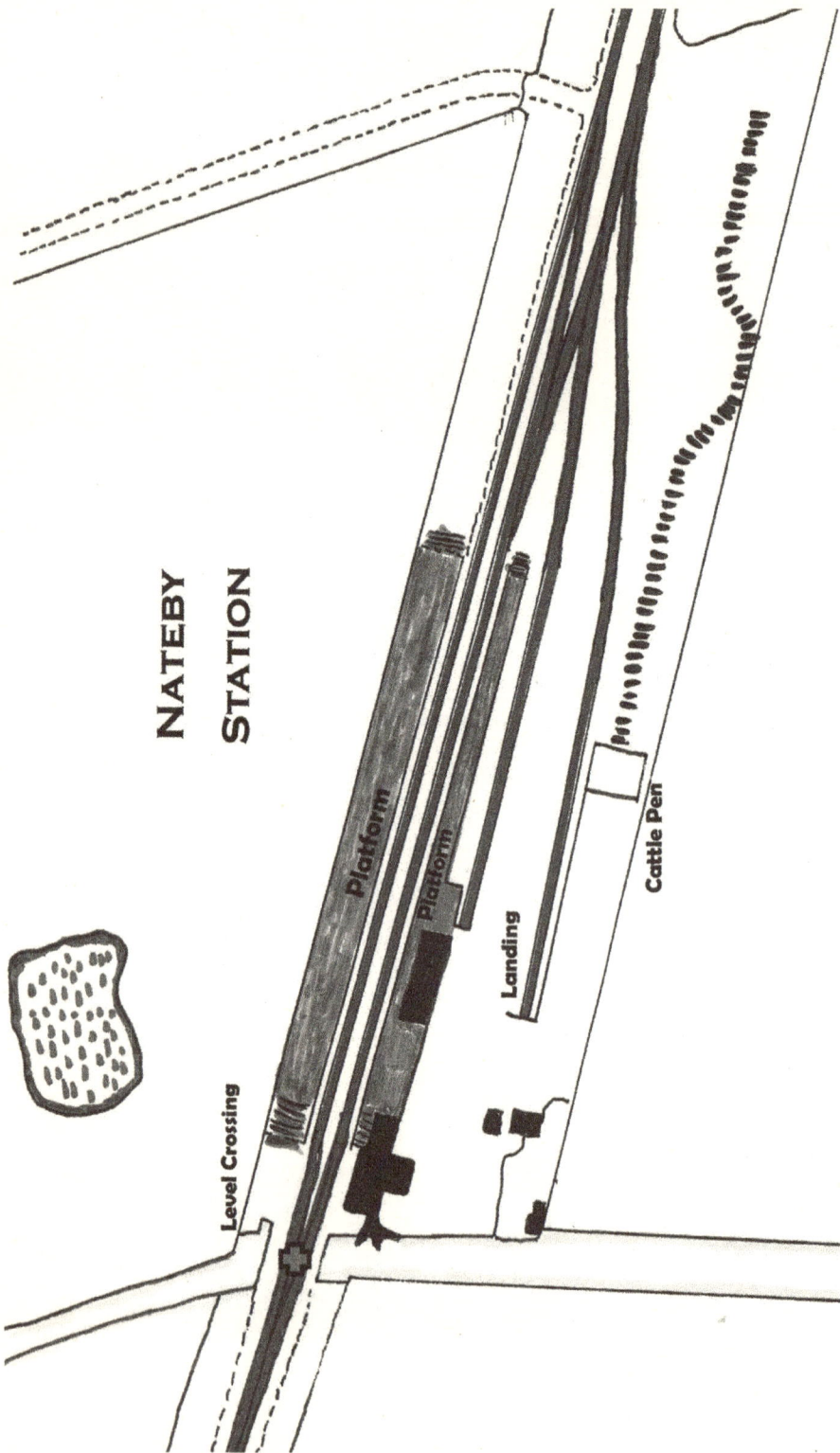

NATEBY STATION

Level Crossing

Platform

Platform

Landing

Cattle Pen

Nateby Station. A plan drawn from an early 20th Century Ordnance Survey Map

Pilling Station. A painting from an old postcard

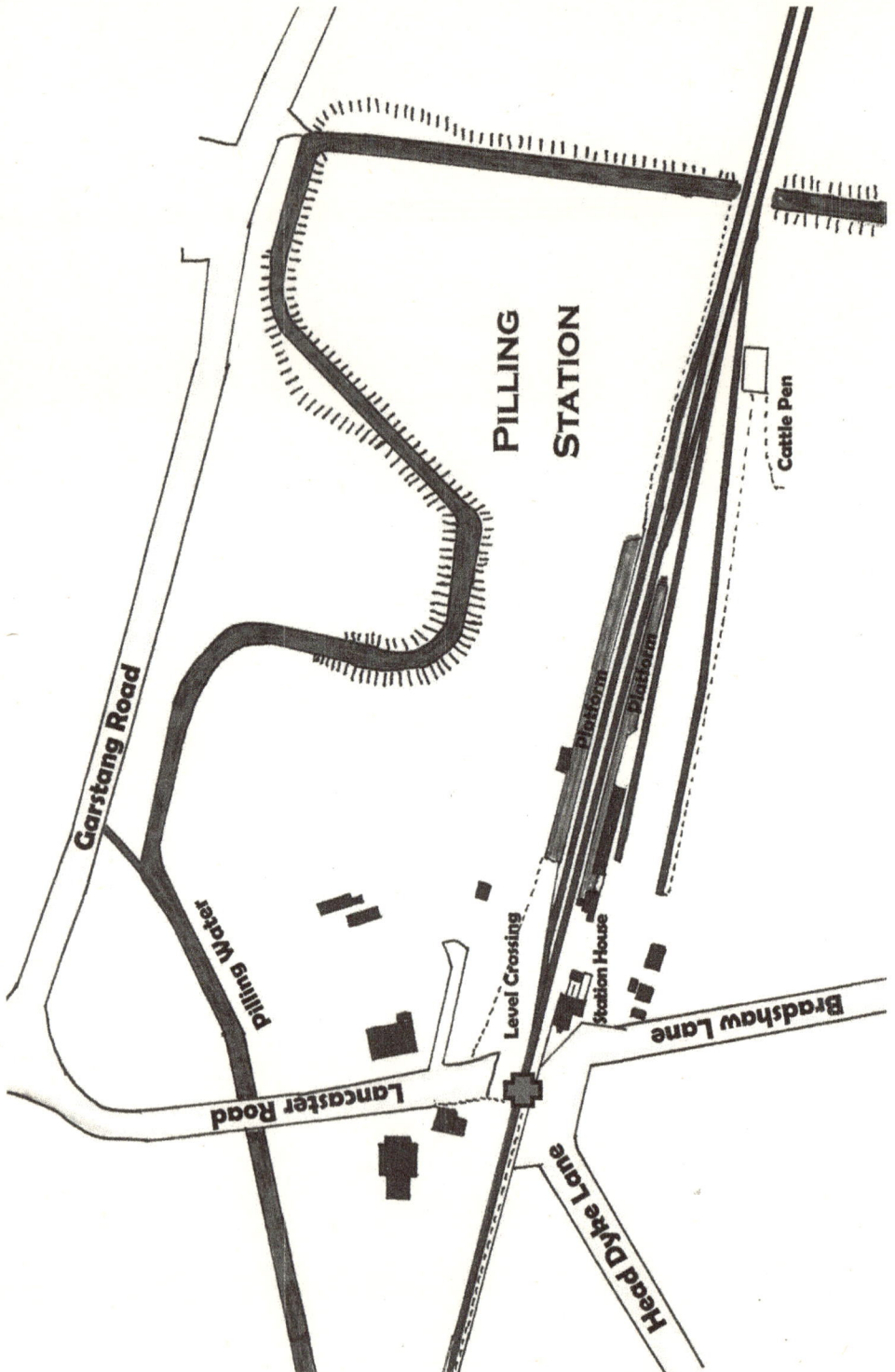

Pilling Station. A plan drawn from an early 20th Century Ordnance Survey Map

Preesall Station. A painting from an old postcard

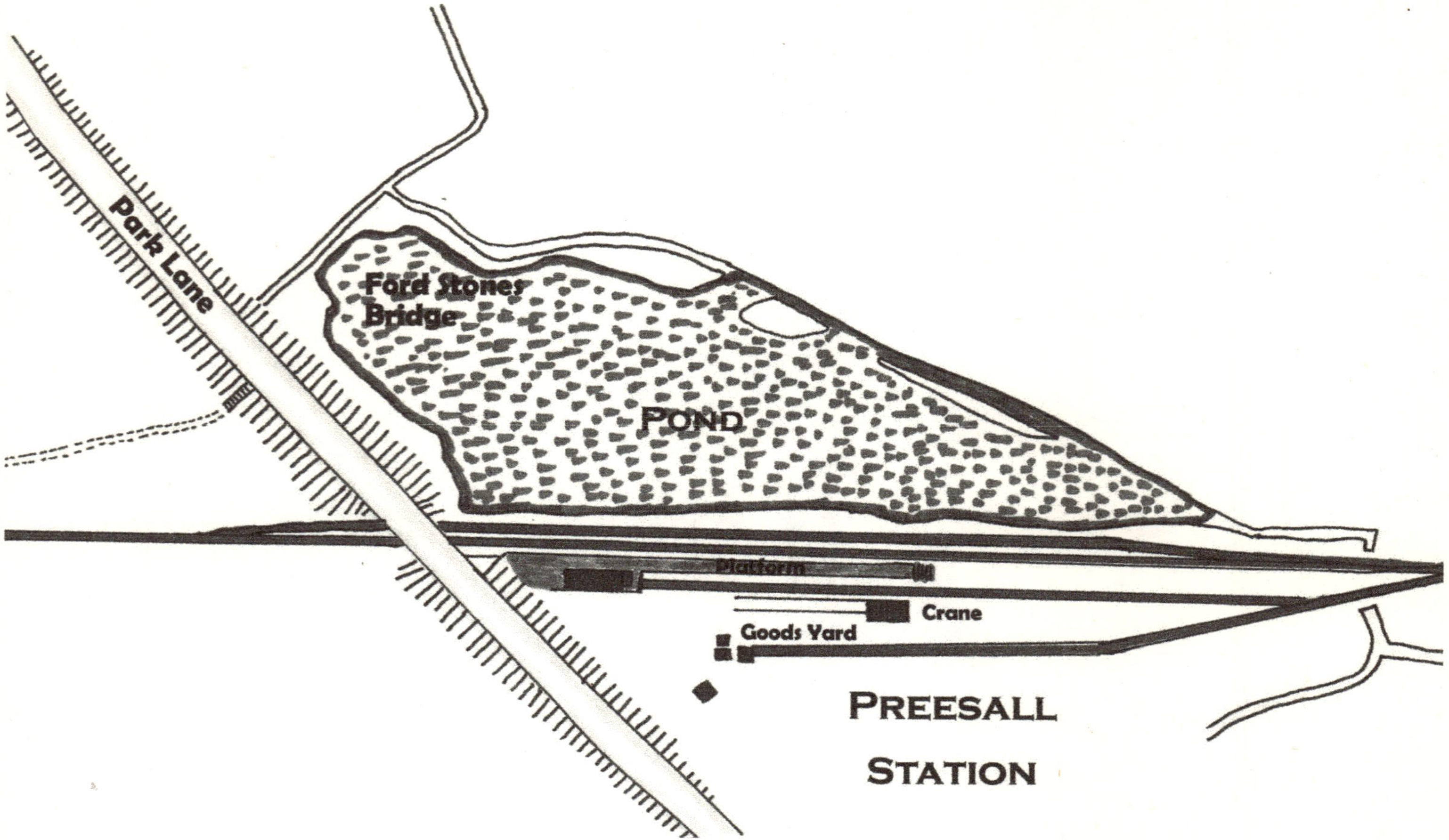
Park Lane
Ford Stones Bridge
POND
Platform
Crane
Goods Yard
PREESALL
STATION

Preesall Station. A plan drawn from an early 20th Century Ordnance Survey Map

Knott End Station. A painting from an old postcard

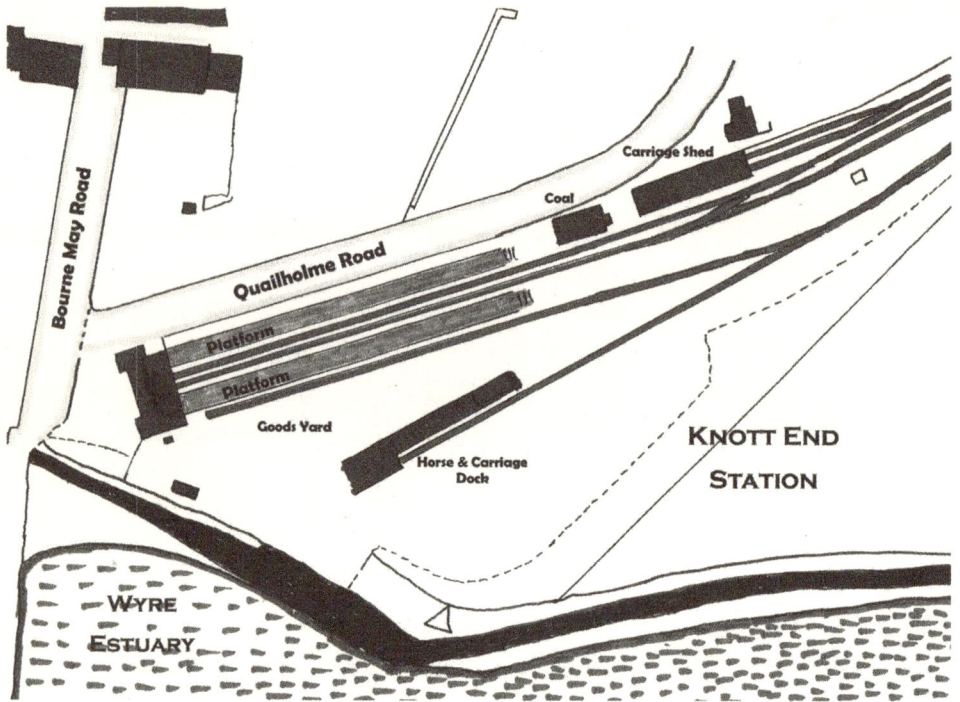

Knott End Station. A plan drawn from an early 20th Century Ordnance Survey Map

Laying the track for the Knott End Railway

Two views of Nateby Station. Photographer unknown.
Below, Garstang Station about 1906. Blackpool Times photograph

Top two picture are Pilling Station. Bottom one is Preesall Station. From old postcards.

An old photograph of the first engine on the line "Hebe". Photo Gazette.

The new carriages supplied for the 1908 extension to Knott End. Picture 1 is the first class carriage, 2 passenger brake van and 3 goods brake van. Photographer not known.

Disaster & Recovery

So it was full steam ahead, or not as it turned out. In the first shareholders' meeting in February 1871 very little was discussed apart from Mr Gardner, the chairman, resigning from the board of directors, due to ill health. In April there was a notice in the press that "Much disappointment was caused on this line of railway on Tuesday, by the 10.30 train which should have met the 10.46 to Preston at the junction, being stopped at Garstang in consequence of the engine breaking down. The traffic on the line was stopped until Wednesday morning, when the engine being repaired the usual trains commenced running." The strain on the engine and the lack of funds were having a severe effect on the railway's operations. This was clearly demonstrated in a report in the Preston Chronicle of 27th January 1872, titled 'Railway Burlesque.'

"The little line called the Garstang and Knot End Railway is the greatest burlesque, the funniest and maddest farce of a concern in England. It may be a railway in somebody's day; but at present it is worse than a mixed up corduroy road with a bad squirrel track at the end of it. The man who said it was easy to get a wife, but an awful job to get furniture, was right in many ways; it is an easy thing to meet at the Royal Oak here, to call for glasses of gin, to sup them, to go into another room, and then say 'We'll have a railway;' but what a business it has been the working out of this affair. I well recollect the meeting at which it was decided to have a railway; at which statements were made about docks at Knott End, about Irish and American trade, a through route into Yorkshire, and dividends which only needed winking at to blossom into fortunes. The promoters got their bill; but the working out of the affair, the 'furniture' part of the job has been a torture, the end of which is not yet. The line, all the way from its junction to that God-forsaken field at Pilling in which it ends, is a tin-pot, ramshackle, twopence halfpenny affair; the rails are of the tin-pot order; the sleepers smell of Yankeeism and poverty; the embankments are half finished as if they did not know whether to ask for an earthquake to swallow them up and relieve them of their misery, or tumble upon the line and close it up; the 'chairs,' and bolts, and rods, and bars, and spikes will find no rest until some dealer in old metal comes round; the station buildings are fitter for some place beyond the Rocky Mountains, where men live in shanties, than in a civilised country; the motive power consists of a kind of Connecticut ballast engine which is worked to death for nothing, and breaks down nearly every day. It broke down this week, terrified several folk, and, if luck had not stepped in, would have seriously scalded one or two men who are not just yet prepared to quit this earthly scene. There seems to be no real manager, no master, no Robinson Crusoe, no man Friday, no anything an this sad, silly little railway; and the supposition is, that in a short time it will be left altogether, and told to look after itself. At the chief station on the line, Garstang Station, in nineteen cases out of twenty one only finds a youth or two, able to do everything except grow whiskers and be civil. The concern is without a manager; and if you find fault with anything, however well founded the case may be, the simple answer is 'can't be helped.' Parcels have to wait hours at this station, in the office, on the ground, on the platform, anywhere, before they are delivered. Seriously speaking the whole line is a bungle-a poor, miserable farce. The company do nothing to cultivate traffic, do everything by indifference, and allowing anybody and everybody to be masters, to disgust people with the concern. There is no certainty about its trains,

because there is none about the vital mechanism of the road, all is either poor or out of joint. There is no satisfaction in dealing with the company because there is no controlling head. The entire affair is a burlesque. We had better get a canal cut down to Pilling, and teach people to swim there and back with there goods. It would be recreation, if nothing else, and we like recreation in this quarter, we do, for sure."

At the end of February a meeting of shareholders was held and the press were excluded, which was regarded as very unusual. The press did manage to get some details of the accounts which showed that a total of further expenditure, still required for line still in the course of construction, was £8,790. The revenue for the half year ending December 31st was £803 with a total mileage for passenger, goods and mineral trains of 10,420. The debts were showing as £17,854. The buildings and the line were certified as being maintained in good condition by John Noble who was managing the line on behalf of the contractors. The plant, engine and carriages were certified by Matthew Sutton, Locomotive Superintendent.

A notice was posted at Garstang Town station at the beginning of March, 1872 to the effect that all traffic would be suspended from Monday 11th March until Wednesday 13th March. While the engine was thoroughly repaired (locomotive expenditure in the half year to December, 1871 were given as £276 13s 9d). The line resumed, but not for long. At the end of March the line closed. Just before this the contractors, Mr Noble and Mr Addie had attended a meeting of their creditors, at the office of Mr Turner, solicitor of Fox Street, Preston, to account for their failure. The creditors resolved that their affairs should be liquidated by arrangement and not in bankruptcy.

On the 27th April, 1872 a report appeared in the Preston Herald.

"It is with a sense of profound emotion that we record the demise or sudden collapse of the G&KER, or, what is truly termed among select circles The Garstang and Knot End Farce. The enterprise was hailed triumphantly when first commenced, but gradually it sickened, and now, in the second year of its existence it has ignominiously expired, and lies mouldering in the grave. The engine has lost its vitality, and is to be seen at the Garstang and Catterall Junction covered with a tarpaulin. It has, however, attached to it a waggon of coals, apparently enjoying the idea that on some future day it will rise from the dead and enjoy a long run of prosperity, and do honour to its maker and masters. We walked over the line this week, and from end to end we found it entirely deserted. The rails are rusty, the rolling stock fast decaying, the station houses very dilapidated; indeed, they may be fitly compared with the ruins of Greenock Castle, as viewed from the road running below it. The only things we failed to inspect were the finances of the company, which we may surmise very much resemble every other feature of the undertaking. To a certain extent this stoppage of operations has slightly inconvenienced a small clique of farmers and others trading at Garstang. An enterprising fellow at Garstang known by the name of 'Bob the Barber,' observing with sorrow the downfall of this amateur railway, has now determined to meet the trains on Thursdays with his conveyance and horse, and carry as many as he can. The trap was soon filled by many notabilities in the potato trade, who we understand have taken up shares in the undertaking. We learned that the stipulated fare was 8d there and back,

and a shave included. Let us hope that this undertaking will be far more profitable than the lamented railway. We are given to understand that on market days a bus has been run from Pilling to Garstang ever since the line was stopped."

In November, 1872 an application for leave to bring in a bill in the 1873 Parliamentary session was placed in the local press. This was to revive the powers to compulsory purchase of lands and extend the time for the completion of the works. This was to allow the company to sell or lease the line.

The bill was debated at the Select Committee of the House of Commons, in March, 1873 and was opposed by the London and North Western Railway Company together with Messrs Galbraith & Tolme, who had been the engineers for the G&KER. The Preston Chronicle took a sceptical view of the LNWR and made a strong comment in the 1st March edition (see clip).

Mr John Noble, the secretary of the company, was called and gave evidence of the history of the venture. He said the whole of the land required for the completion of the line had been bought and nearly the whole of it had been paid for. The company had now no money, and unless the bill was passed, would not be able to complete the line. Mr Aspinall on behalf of the LNWR said his clients had a very strong feeling in this matter, and if the committee passed the proposed bill they would afford a precedent which was unwarranted by past legislation. The line from its commencement seemed to be a contractor's line of the worst character and the company were without money and without stock. The bill was rejected.

> The London and North Western Railway Company quaking! Who would have thought that this gigantic company with it millions of revenue per annum, the most colossal in the world, now that the East India Company is extinct, would have been compelled to express its trepidation before an unexpectant and dismayed world? Yet such is the fact. The Leviathan of the Railway Interests is pouring out its direful wailings and forebodings before the Public Works Committee of the House of Commons, and the special subject of its alarm is the competition it is likely to meet with from—the Garstang and Knot End Railway! They have positively petitioned against the proposed sale of the Garstang and Knot End line, on the ground that, if it gets into the hands of nobody knows who, the London and North Western may suffer greatly from the competition! Really this amounts to something "new under the sun"—to something about as new as would be the information that the biggest ostrich in the Royal Zoological Gardens had fainted at the sight of a tom-tit, or that the maternal hippopotamus therein had become alarmed at the attitude of a stray half-starved white mouse.

Also in March there were rumors in the press that the Midland Railway Company had purchased the line.

In November, 1873 a new application was made to Parliament to bring in a bill with the object of authorizing a sale by or under the Court of Chancery, or otherwise by auction, or by private contract, or otherwise, of the undertaking, railway works, and other property, estate, and effects...of the Garstang and Knot End Railway Company. One of the powers was also to provide, if necessary or expedient, for the dissolution of the Company and the winding up of its affairs.

An official receiver was appointed and guided the debenture holders (the people who had lent the money) to re-start the process of getting the railway ready for accepting traffic. The engine Hebe, which had been on hire, had been taken back due to non-payment and a new engine was required.

In the Preston Chronicle of 15th August, 1874 was an article which described a journey on the line before it closed.

"It was one bright morning, about the beginning of June, when we, along with three other equally inquisitive sight-seers, proceeded to Pilling for the sake of its gulls; and at that time the Garstang and Knot End Railway was in working order, a living, breathing affair, not a dead, rail rusted, grass grown concern, to smile at and wonder about, as it is now. In about 25 minutes after leaving Preston, we were at the Garstang and Catterall; and a move of a few yards, after leaving the main station there, brought us to a train standing on parallel rails, whose destination was the arcadian land of Pilling. Now the train was of a curious kind, made up of a couple of elongated, Yankee-looking carriages, something like a pair of new omnibuses pulled out to three times their regular length, whilst at the front there was a fanciful little engine which looked more like a mechanical toy than anything intended for pulling big carriages or heavy waggons. That engine was in the habit of breaking down, through over strain, about three times a week; but, somehow, it always came up smiling again, ready for any storm, and on this particular morning it seemed as full of "go" and courage as a prize bantam. We got into one of the carriages, the entrance being at the end, without a ticket; others followed suit; and for a few minutes time was whiled away in looking at its interior and at the little line it was made for. It seemed like an elephant on a squirrel track, so big was its form in comparison with the size of the line. Directly after the train started, a young man in official garb, went to one corner of the carriage, unlocked a box (this was the booking office), gave out tickets, and took pay for them. By-and-bye, we wound round the ruined pile of Greenhalgh Castle; then got to Garstang station; and then ahead over a long stretch of flat land, until finally we arrived at Pilling station. The railway stopped here; the rails ran into a field as if anxious to go forward somewhere, but unable to come to any conclusion on the subject. A facetious writer once said that this railway was called the Knot End line because it did not end. On leaving Pilling station we made inquiry for the "Gull Island," that being the name of the place where the gulls most do congregate in Pilling..."

All through 1874 and into 1875 an action had been taking place in the full Court of Exchequer between Messrs Galbraith and Tolme, the engineers and the Railway Company for recovery of professional charges incurred by them as engineers in charge of obtaining the Acts of Parliament and overseeing the construction of the railway. In the end the judgement went against them.

Towards the end of the year reports started appearing in the press charting the progress of the restoration. In October, 1874 the Preston Chronicle said, "We understand that the G&KER, which was a failure to the original company, has been undertaken by a number of influential gentlemen and Mr Wardley, of Preston, is now superintending the repairs of the line, which it is expected will be open to the public in the course of a fortnight or three weeks. An engine for the company has already been purchased." In the Lancaster Gazette of the 14th November "A number of workmen are employed upon the permanent way of the G&KER making the necessary repairs. The matter is being prosecuted with vigour." Also in the Lancaster Gazette of 14th December, 1874 "A first journey was made upon this line under the new proprietors, but it was not very successful. Stakepool was made alright, but on the return journey an accident befell the engine. Believed to be occasioned by a scarcity of water, which retarded its further progress. Thus the operations were delayed."

The engine which was purchased was called Union. It was a second hand engine, built in1868 by Manning Wardle. It was a 0-4-0 saddle tank used by a contractor named James Pilling in the construction of the Lancashire Union Railway.

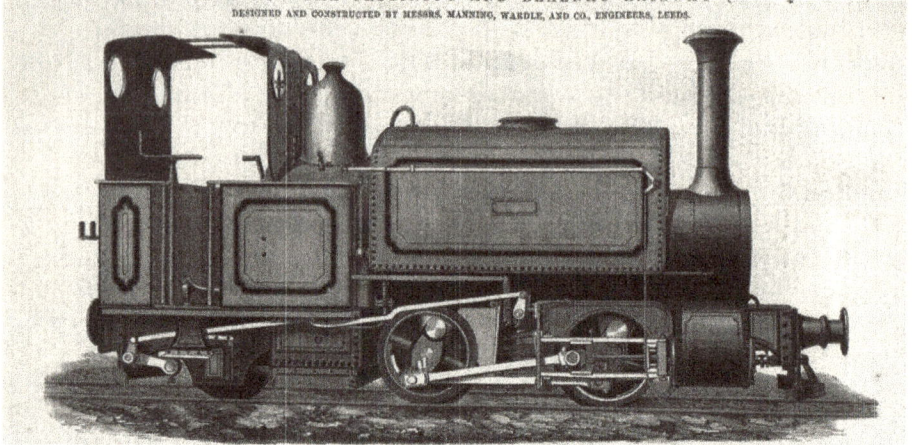

DESIGNED AND CONSTRUCTED BY MESSRS. MANNING, WARDLE, AND CO., ENGINEERS, LEEDS.

An advertisement for a locomotive similar to "Union" manufactured by Manning Wardle & Co. Illustration courtesy of Grace's Guide to British Industrial History.

At the shareholder's meeting at the end of February, 1875, it was announced that the debenture holders had placed an engine on the line, and that goods traffic had now been resumed. A strong feeling was expressed in favour of passenger trains also being run. The directors said it was in contemplation, but they looked for some assistance from parties residing in the district, who would be benefitted by the opening of the line, towards the purchase of a second engine, which would be required. One gentleman present stated his willingness to find the necessary funds for another engine.

The line was re-opened to goods traffic on the 23rd February, 1875 and for passenger traffic on the 17th April. Another company was formed on the 9th December, 1875, called the Garstang & Knott End Railway Engine Company, and they purchased another engine called Farmers' Friend, which they hired to the railway reputably for £116 a year. In the Preston Herald of 12th December it was reported that "On Monday last the first trial trip of a new engine, manufactured by Messrs Hudswell, Clark, and Rodgers, Railway Foundry, Leeds, took place on this

railway. The engine went down to Pilling in first rate style, and evidently gave satisfaction." The engine was a 0-6-0 saddle tank which was said to have a piercing whistle which got it the nickname the "Pilling Pig." Another explanation for the name was given when the closure of passenger services was announced in the Lancashire Evening Post on the 10th March, 1930. "One of the earliest engines on the line was the 'Farmers' Friend,' a diminutive locomotive which snorted and puffed so noisily, and progressed so slowly that it was dubbed the 'Pilling Pig,' a name which has stuck to all succeeding engines except one-the last."

The line started to prosper and at a meeting in February 1877, with Major Mounsey in the chair, the accounts from December, 1875 to December, 1876 showed an increase in passenger numbers of 12,593, of minerals 594 tons and general merchandise 2,548 tons.

By 1881 the Company, albeit very slowly, was making a little headway in paying off their debt and bringing the line and properties up to standard. At a meeting in August the Chairman, Dr Chapman, said that when the new directors came into power they found the permanent way in very bad order, with rotten sleepers and bad rails, and they had to spend every farthing they had in hand on making good the road and repairing the engine. They were now in the process of trying to agree with the debenture holder a way to re-organize the debt. They were also still thinking of the completion of the line to Knott End and made an application to Parliament in 1882 to revive the powers and extend the time for the purchase of land and construction of works. They also wanted to raise additional capital, make arrangements with creditors and convert debentures into debenture stock. Gradually the rolling stock debt was taken over by the company and in January, 1884, the Garstang Rolling Stock Company was dissolved.

In 1884 another locomotive was acquired for the railway via the Railway Engine Company. It was purchased from Hudswell, Clarke and Company and was an 0-6-0 saddle tank engine called "Hope." The engine "Union" was taken in part exchange. In the August, 1884 half-year accounts, hire of locomotives, "Farmers' Friend" and "Hope," are charged at £124 12s.

An advertisement for Hudswell, Clarke & Co. Courtesy of Grace's Guide to British Industrial History

The Garstang & Knott End Railway was now a going concern and was able to purchase "Farmers' Friend" from the Engine Company. It paid for this over a number of years from receipts, with the final payment at the end of 1889. The number of passengers was steady at about 20,000 first and third class each half year, but the amount of goods carried was increasing steadily. The main problem seemed to be a shortage of goods wagons as shown by this report in the Preston Herald of 15 February, 1890.

"The fatality at Pilling station.-At the Preston Infirmary, on Thursday, an inquest was held by the Coroner (Dr. Gilbertson) upon the body of Robert Bradshaw, a potato dealer, of Fisher's Road, Pilling, who died in that institution on the previous day from injuries received through having been run over on The Garstang and Knott End Railway on Tuesday last. The evidence went to show that deceased was in the habit of watching trains arrive at the Pilling Station, running along the side of a wagon and jumping in before the train had stopped. This he did for the purpose of securing a wagon for the conveyance of his potatoes, as there was a scarcity of wagons on the line. On Tuesday he was seen running alongside a wagon, a practice he had been cautioned about, when he stumbled just as he was about to spring into it. He at first fell by the side of the train, but in trying to get up he got onto the line, and several of the wagons passed over his legs. He was as quickly as possible removed to the Preston Infirmary, where he succumbed to his injuries. A verdict of accidental death was returned."

In the accounts for the half year ending June 1887, there was a large charge of £292 for "Farmers' Friend" being sent back to the manufacturers in Leeds for major repairs. There was also an increase in general charges due to the fact that the Court of Chancery had allowed the manager and receiver four years remuneration for their services and expenses. In the Lancaster Gazette of 9th October, 1889 was an editorial comment on the philosophy of the management of the railway.

"The Garstang and Knott End Railway with its Farmers' Friend locomotive is an institution possessed of a curious constitution. I met a metropolitan gentleman a few nights ago who had been to Pilling, and who stated that on returning to Pilling Station he wondered why the train of the G&KER did not depart at the proper time. On asking the youth in charge of the booking department he received the laconic and self-satisfied reply: "O, sir, we never run our trains on time on this line." I have known the G&KER train stop to oblige a farmer running and whistling across the fields from Winmarleigh in order to travel to Garstang, just as if this train were a tram car. But then the engine is called the Farmers' Friend, and when I found this out I ceased to wonder at the obliging nature of those of those in charge of this quaint conveyance."

So a new decade dawned and the railway still only went as far as Pilling after twenty years. For most of the early part of the decade the company trundled slowly along. It made some money, but never a lot. There just were not enough passengers to make it prosperous. At a meeting in August, 1891, the subject of the continuation of the line to Knott End was brought up and one of the shareholders asked how long they had left, on the existing legislation, to finish the extension. The answer was seven years taking it to 1898. It was put forward that the extension would be good for business and would make the railway pay, but again there was shortage of money. The shareholders were getting restless and in July, 1992 there was another meeting at the Royal Oak, in Garstang, to discuss the proposed extension. The chairman, Dr. Chapman, told the meeting that ten years previously the managers found the line in a state which was utterly unsuitable for an engine to run on, and it was without adequate fences, rails, sleepers and necessary equipment. Out of the revenue they had spent something over £10,000 in providing new stock and equipment. The revenue had increased and they had a nice balance in the bank and when the line was completed it would give a boost to Fleetwood, Knott End and their revenues. Pilling folks especially, would be glad to see the last four miles of their railway completed. The Salt Co. at Preesall wanted the line to pass by the south side of Preesall Hill and it was thought they had made a good offer. Mr Addie said that he thought if they could raise £6,000 that would be sufficient to complete the line for goods and mineral traffic. This would raise the revenue of the company and would enable them to go to Parliament for powers to open the line for passenger traffic. It was decided to form a committee to look into ways of raising the money.

At the next meeting in August, 1892, it was proposed "that the directors be instructed to request Mr R Finch, of the firm of Finch and Johnson, Preston, to give the necessary notice of their intention to deposit and promote a bill for powers to raise the necessary capital to complete the line, and to confirm a scheme for the consolidation of the stocks of the company."

It was also proposed "that Mr Augustus Strongitharm, civil engineer, of Barrow, be appointed engineer to the company, with instructions to look over the lines and make an estimate of the amount required to complete and equip the line."

These proposals do not seem to have progressed and the meetings over the next few years were badly attended with just the balance sheets being published. In August, 1893 it was announced that the company had built a new shed and made a new platform at Cogie Hill for the convenience of the residents of Winmarleigh and Eagland Hill. £797 profit was made for the half year.

In February, 1895, another good profit of £849 for the half year was reported. The general manager, the assistant manager, and the goods manager of the London and North Western Railway Company travelled over the line and inspected the track to and from Knott End. It was said the residents of the district attached considerable significance to the visit. By August, 1896 the business had slumped a little. Part of the problem was the decrease in the price of potatoes, they did not realise more than 2s 6d a load.

In August, 1897, it was announced that they had bought a new engine. This was a Hudswell Clarke 0-6-0 saddle tank engine named "Jubilee Queen" in honour of Queen Victoria's diamond jubilee. The engine "Hope" was taken in part exchange and due to this the Garstang & Knott End Railway Company was dissolved in October, 1898. A proposal was made for a scheme for the reorganization of the company. By that means they would free themselves from the Court of Chancery, which was a very great burden.

By 1898 a new company had been formed, The Knott End Railway Company. In March a bill came before Parliament to complete the line of the railway from Pilling to Knott End. In opposition were The Garstang and Knot End Company and the Quail Home Estate. After stating the advantages to the line attention was turned to the Quail Home Estate objections. The objection reduced itself to a question of two bridges which the promoters saw no need for. After a discussion it was decided that one bridge would be provided, which cleared the objection. The engineer of the line, Mr Edward Seaton, provided evidence as did other interested parties. The committee adjourned for the night, and when the session commenced the next day Mr Wedderburn, for the promoters, announced that since the preceding night an agreement had been made between the Garstang and Knot End Company and the proposed company and the effect of this was the objection had been withdrawn. The new Company proposed to purchase the Garstang and Knot End Company. The bill was passed and the Knott End Railway Company was incorporated on the 12 August, 1898.

On the 17th October, 1898 a prospectus was issued.

Issue at Par of £50,000 in 10,000 shares of £5 each. Payable 10s on application, £2 10s on allocation, £1 after three months and £1 after six months.

The Knott End Railway Company has been incorporated by Act of Parliament (the Knott End Railway Act, 1898) for the purpose of constructing, working and maintaining a railway from Pilling to Knot End, near Fleetwood, Lancashire, plan of which is enclosed herewith.

The terminus of the railway is situate on the northern bank of the River Wyre, immediately opposite the important town and harbour of Fleetwood, from which there is an excellent service of steamers sailing between the Isle of Man, Barrow and Ireland, and will be in direct communication from Fleetwood with Blackpool by the new Electric Tramway.

By the construction of this line the distance from Lancaster and the North to Fleetwood and to the Isle of Man via Fleetwood will be shortened by eighteen miles, and a saving in time on present timetables of from one to two hours; and there is no doubt a very large number of passengers will avail themselves of this short route. Blackpool is connected with Fleetwood not only by railway, but by an electric tramway, which was opened for traffic on July 14th last.

During the short period which has elapsed since the opening of the Blackpool and Fleetwood Electric Tramroad the returns have proved most satisfactory, as will be seen by the following figures which have been supplied by the Company.

Number of passengers carried from 14th July to 26th September, 1898, inclusive. 515,654.

Amount of Revenue from the above named traffic. £11,269.

The tramroad was not fully equipped with cars for the present season, and the Company have not, therefore, been able to cope with the traffic. Thousands of passengers have been unable to obtain seats on the tram cars, both at Blackpool and Fleetwood, and arrangements are now being made by which the number of cars will be increased from 10 to 27 for next season. As an illustration of the value of local investments it might be mentioned that the £10 Shares in this Company are quoted at £15.

The ferry between Fleetwood and Knott End is now worked by the Fleetwood Urban District Council, and during the half year just concluded over 314,800 tickets for passengers have been issued, and a contract for the construction of a new steamer for the ferry service has been sealed. It is also proposed to further alter and improve the ferry landing stage at Knott End, in view of the passenger and other traffic from this new railway, whose terminus is immediately adjoining the Knott End Ferry.

The number of annual visitors to Blackpool has been computed at over 3,000,000 and to the Isle of Man at half a million, and it is considered that a large number of these visitors will make use of this Railway, if only for the purpose of affording them access to the beautiful mountain scenery lying to the east of Garstang, the Pilling Sands, and the old fashioned village of Garstang.

The Railway will be constructed at first as a single line, and of the ordinary gauge, with 56lb rails, so as to enable the goods traffic to and from the London and North Western Railway or other systems to be carried to its destination without transhipment. The Act confers running powers over the Garstang and Knot End Railway in order to join the main line of the London and North Western Railway . The company have entered into an Agreement dated 28th April, 1898 to purchase the undertaking of the Garstang and Knott End Railway, subject to the sanction of Parliament, so that then the Company will own a railway eleven miles in length, in direct communication with the main line of the London and North Western Railway, with the joint use of the Garstang and Catterall Station of that Company.

The Directors are of the opinion that the local traffic, including the carriage of market produce to Fleetwood and Blackpool and bricks and building materials to Knott End, will be sufficient to make the line remunerative, and in support of this it may be pointed out that the Garstang and Knot End Railway carried in 1897 upwards of 40,000 passengers and earned a revenue of nearly £4,000, although that Railway has no connection with either Fleetwood or Blackpool.

The extreme fertility of the district through which the line passes, will make the carriage of produce to the markets of Fleetwood and Blackpool an important item in the revenue of the undertaking.

An agreement has been made between the Company and the Urban Distict Council of Fleetwood whereby the Company has obtained facilities of an exceptionally favourable character from the Council with respect to the traffic across the ferry. The Directors also propose to arrange with the Tramway Company for through bookings from Blackpool to all stations on the Company's line.

The Directors have entered into important arrangements with the United Alkali Company, who have large works at Preesall and Fleetwood, for the provision of sidings and other accommodation for the Company, so that traffic may be carried over this railway. The Directors are assured that a considerable revenue will be derived from this source.

An agreement has also been entered into, dated October 4th, 1898, between this

Company of the one part, and Robert Worthington of the other part, providing for the payment of all expenses in connection with the present issue of capital up to date of allotment, the purchase of the land and the delivery to the Company of the single line fully completed by December 31st, 1899, for the sum of £34,000.

Application for shares should be made on the form enclosed with the Prospectus, and sent, with remittance for the amount payable on application, to the Bankers of the Company. In case no allotment is made to any applicant the deposit will be returned in full, or should the shares allotted be less than the number applied for, the surplus deposit will be credited in reduction of the amount payable on allotment.

Directors
The Rt. Hon. Lord Greville, Chairman, Director of the Central Ireland Railway.
H Chandos Elletson, Esq., Parrox Hall, Preesall.
Ernest Crosby, Esq., Solicitor, Fleetwood.
Col. Macnaghten, The Briars, Shortlands.
Bankers. The Manchester & County Bank, Ltd., Fleetwood.
Solicitors. Messrs Baker, Lees & Co., 72 Great George Street, London, S.W.
Engineers. James B Walton, Esq., M.I.C.E., 6 Great College Street, Westminster, S.W.
Messrs Garlick & Sykes, M.I.C.E., Blackpool
Secretary. Mr Arthur Barlow

PARROX HALL, PREESALL, KNOTT END-ON-SEA.

An old postcard of Parrox Hall where one of the directors of the Knott End Railway Company lived. The railway was to pass immediately behind the Hall on its way from Knott End to Preesall.

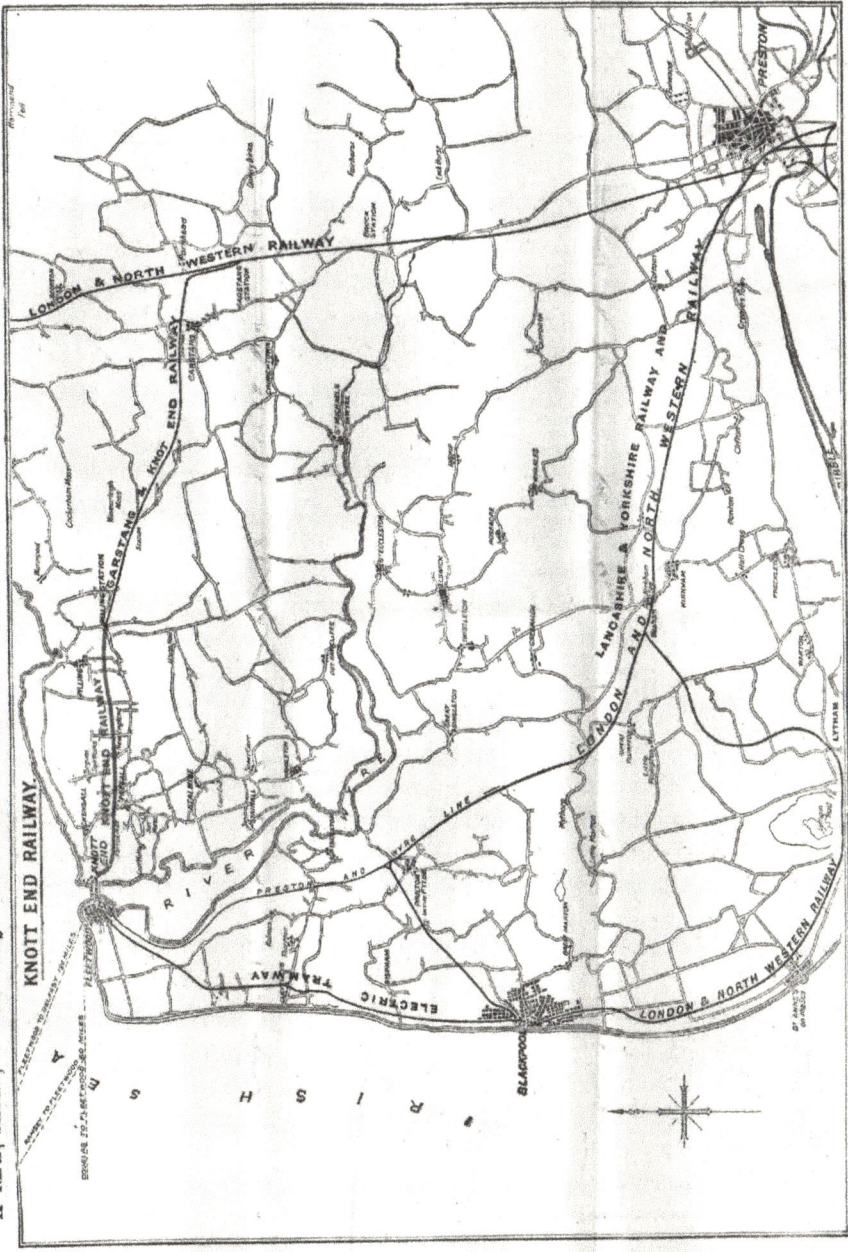

A NEW, SHORT, & PICTURESQUE ROUTE TO & FROM BLACKPOOL, & THE ISLE OF MAN FROM THE NORTH OF ENGLAND.

This is a map of the proposed extension to the existing line that was supplied with the 1898 Prospectus. It shows the advantages of the shorter route from the north as against the other available routes via Preston.

Final stages of construction.

On Wednesday the 25th January, 1899, in perfect weather, Sir Matthew White Ridley, M.P., Home Secretary and Member of Parliament for Blackpool, cut the first sod of the extension of the Garstang and Knot End Railway from Stakepool to Knott End. It was attended by many distinguished guests and members of the public. The spade with which he made the cut was presented to him by Mr R Worthington, of Dublin, the contractor, who had it made for the occasion. The blade, which was inscribed, was solid silver and the handle was ebony and made by West & Son, College Green, Dublin.

In the report in the Preston Herald were a couple of interesting items. The first, when referring to the name Knott End, pondered: *"It will probably still be known as Knott End for many years to come, though efforts have been made to induce the world to look upon the little watering place as St Bernards-on-the-Sea. The efforts have not been particularly successful so far, but we do not know what the case may be as the years roll by."*

The party returned across the Wyre to the Mount Hotel for lunch, which is the other interesting item. *"The menu was as follows:- Hors d'oeuvres varies, clear mock turtle soup a la Reine, sauman en mayonnaise, soles enaspic, pate de pigeon a la Lucullus, capon farcie auz truffles, galantine de dindon, jambon de York, poulet roti, salade de homard , pate de fois gras de Strasbourg, galantine de boeuf, faisine, gele au vin de champagne, crème a la vanilla, meringue glace, gele au kirsch, ananas, fraise, raisin, etc.*

At the shareholders' meeting of the Garstang & Knot End Co., in February 1899, after announcing the death of the late secretary of the company, Mr John Noble, it was reported that the receipts had improved and were almost ten per cent up on the year before. There was an item, headed locomotive power, of £1499. This was for a new engine that had been paid for out of revenue. The engine was called "New Century," and was a 0-6-0 saddle tank engine from Hudswell, Clarke & Co. "Farmers' Friend," was taken in part exchange.

A further prospectus was issued in 1899 which contained some extra information.

"A contract for the construction of the Railway has been entered into with Mr Robert Worthington, who has had a large experience in railway construction. The works are now in progress, and will, the Directors are informed, be completed before the end of the year. The Directors were favoured by the Rt. Hon. Sir Matthew White Ridley most kindly cutting the first sod on the 25th January last, and, as the enclosed extracts from the newspaper accounts of the ceremony show, the Directors are glad to learn not only that the proposed Railway will supply a long felt want, but that it is widely believed that it will prove a commercial success.

This belief is further confirmed by the following report submitted to them by their Consulting Engineer, Sir Douglas Fox, Vice President Inst. C. E., after careful personal inspection and enquiries. Dated January 31st 1899 the report is very favourable and concludes.

"The increasing building operation on your line, and the extension of the Alkali Works, should greatly assist your Company's traffic, while the new line will pass through one of the richest agricultural districts of the Fylde. The Garstang market is a poor one, and the farmers and others upon the open line will now be brought into close touch with the Fleetwood market.

If efficiently worked in harmonious relations with the companies at either end, I consider that your railway should yield substantial dividends to the shareholders."

Copies of press reports of the first sod cutting were included with this prospectus.

An intriguing item appeared in the Preston Herald of 31st May, 1899. This was headed, "The Proposed Light Railway, Knott End extension to Lancaster." It was an application, by the Knott End Railway Company, to the Light Railway Commissioners for an order to authorize the construction, maintenance and working of a light railway between Pilling and Lancaster. It was to go 800 yards west of Pilling Station through Pilling, Wrampool, Cockerham, Thurnham, and Ellel crossing over the canal and the LNW Railway and on through Galgate and into Scotforth a distance of 10 miles, 1 furlong and 7 chains.

The actual work on the new line didn't start until 1900, and the press reported that the work had been resumed with increased vigour. Large quantities of materials had been delivered and quite a lot of the laying out of the line and foundations for the buildings had been done. One of the problems was the agreement, during the Parliamentary committee session, with the Quail Holme Estate to provide a bridge at Preesall. This turned out to be the most difficult engineering work on the line and soon the company were in financial difficulties.

On the 31st May, 1900, an auction was held at Pilling station, by order of the Sheriff, to sell amongst other things 250 tons of new steel 30ft rails, 11 tons fish plates, 3 tons fish bolts, 9 tons dog picks, 350 galvanised posts and a quantity of Accrington bricks.

In a letter to the Lancashire Daily Post, published 29th May, 1900, the solicitor for the contractor pointed out the seizure of the rails and other materials had been made due to a law suit by the solicitors for the company for costs incurred by them and that his client had nothing to do with this. He finished by saying "My client will now take the necessary steps against the company to protect his interests." So the work had now ground to a halt. Meanwhile the Garstang and Knot End Railway Company plodded along, and at the meeting called for August, 1900, not enough shareholders turned up for the meeting and it had to be cancelled. A small profit was recorded on the balance sheet.

In January, 1901, in the Chancery Division, a petition of the Manchester and County Bank, a creditor of the Knott End Railway Company, was heard. Mr Eldon Bankes, who appeared in support of the petition, said "the company was incorporated in 1898 for the purpose of constructing a light railway, and the land had been prepared for a railway and was now ready for ballast. A large quantity of rails had been deposited on the ground, but these had been seized by a judgement creditor. It was hoped that a contractor night be found to carry out the work, and that hereafter it would become a valuable property, but unless the court protected the undertaking by appointing a receiver and manager the line would not be completed, and would ultimately become derelict. After a long argument between numerous counsel for different interests, Mr Ernest Crosby, a solicitor from Fleetwood, was appointed interim receiver.

The working side of the railway scheduled a meeting in February, 1901, but couldn't get anybody interested even though they made a profit for the half year of seven hundred and fifty five pounds. The Preston Herald commented; *"The Garstang and Knot End Railway already satisfies the idea of the curious for it is the second smallest railway in England, but certain events that have occurred add a distinction that no other railway can possibly claim. The shareholders of this miniature company neglected to attend the half yearly meeting convened last August, and they were so little interested in the concern this week that they failed to form a quorum, consequently no business has been transacted for twelve months."*

The Knott End Railway issued a report mid year summarizing the situation.

"Powers to construct a single line of Railway were obtained by The Knott End Railway Act (which received the Royal Assent on the 12th August 1989) from Stake Pool (Pilling), the present terminus of the Garstang Railway, to Knott End at a point adjoining the landing stage of the Knott End Ferry opposite to Fleetwood and which measures 4 miles and 7.70 chains. The time allowed for completion of the works is five years from the passing of the Act i.e. 12th August 1903. The time allowed for compulsory purchase of land expired at the end of three years from the passing of the Act i.e. 12th August 1901.

The total nominal capital of the Company is £50,000 divided into 10,000 shares of £5 each and the Company may (sec. 12) with the authority of thee-fourths of the votes of the shareholders divide any share in their capital into half shares of which one shall be called "preferred half share" and the other "deferred half share" but only when sixty per cent has been paid up on each of the shares it is proposed to divide. The dividend on the "preferred" shares shall be fixed at a rate not exceeding six per cent and is not cumulative.

When the whole of the nominal capital has been issued and accepted and one half (£25,000) has been paid up, and not less than one fifth of the amount of each separate share has been paid up, the Company may borrow on Mortgage of the Undertaking the sum of £15,000.

A contract was arranged with Mr Robert Worthington to provide for payment of all expenses in connection with the issue of the Capital, the purchase of the land and the delivery of the single line fully completed by 31st December 1899 for the sum of £34,000. A Prospectus was issued on 17th October 1898 and a further Prospectus was issued at a later date and £5,955 of the Share Capital was subscribed by the public on which the sum of £5,946 has been paid.

As the Company was short of funds the Contractor by a supplementary contract under which £5,000 was added to his original Contract (making it altogether £39,000) agreed to accept £33,000 in Shares and £6,000 in cash subject to £15,000 of such shares being exchanged for Debenture when the line was completed.

The Contractor received the £6,000 in cash and had allotted to him £14,355 in Shares in respect of work done, when an action against the Company resulted in an execution by the Sheriff who removed rails on the works and put an end to the progress and for two years practically nothing has been done.

The present Directors and officials are nominees of the Contractor and no further progress can be made unless Capital is provided for the Contractor to complete his work. The whole of the land required has not been purchased and in addition to other liabilities part of the shares are we understand deposited at the Bankers as collateral security in connection with a joint & several guarantee by the old Directors.

In November 1901 a notice was posted in the newspapers for renewal of powers, in the 1902 session of Parliament, to revive the Act of 1898 to enable compulsory purchase of lands and completion of the works. Again in November 1902 another similar application was made for the 1903 session of Parliament. At the same time they had an advert in the paper with 70 tons of good second hand FB steels rails and fish plates for sale.

Over the course of several years the apathy at the Garstang & Knot End Railway continued. Most of the meetings were ignored by the shareholders and the directors and just the balance sheets were distributed without any business being conducted. The local press again commented on the lack of interest in the company.

On the 5th July 1904 was an article that gave a glimpse of the future; it said *"A long, long time ago an attempt was made to connect the Lancaster district with the River Wyre, and the Garstang and Knot End railway was commenced. Unfortunately, however, the line never reached Knott End, and since its opening the operations of its single engine and antediluvian coach, known as the Pilling elephant, have been confined to the district between Garstang and Catterall junction and the village of Pilling. Now, what the railway failed to accomplish the motor car has succeeded in doing, and yesterday the first of a series of motor char-a-bancs was put on the road to complete the journey from Pilling to Knott End. Each coach will hold eighteen persons."*

In November 1905 another statutory notice was placed in the newspapers applying to the 1906 session of Parliament for an extension of time for construction and completion of Railway and Works. This passed through Parliament and the time was extended for two years from August 12th, 1906.

During 1907 the finances started to get back on track. Mr Worthington, the contractor from Dublin arranged the financing of the purchase of the Garstang and Knot End Railway Company and the Knott End Railway Company. The chairman of the company was Mr Hugh C Smith, a former Governor of the Bank of England and still a director. He owned considerable property in Fleetwood. There were also negotiations with the

United Alkali Company to discuss the potential for goods traffic. In November, 1907 an application was made, by the Knott End Railway, for the 1908 session in Parliament for construction of new railways in Lancashire plus powers to enable the Company to purchase the undertaking of the Garstang and Knot End Railway Company and provide for the winding up of this company. They also wanted to construct a railway extension from Stakepool to the London and North Western Railway at Ellel, just south of Lancaster. In February, 1908 a meeting of those interested in the Garstang and Knot End Railway was held at Preston and assurances were given that, subject to the terms of arrangement, the bill would be unopposed by this company. It was taken over on the 1st July, 1908. It was purchased for £50,000.

The work on finishing the line started in January, 1908 and proceeded at a fast pace and

An early cartoon re-drawn.

by July was finished.

The formal opening of the line was on the 30th July, 1908. The report in the Manchester Courier of 31st July said; *"Amid local rejoicings the extension of the railway from Pilling to Knott End was opened to the public for the first time yesterday. A train conveying specially invited guests left Knott End, the terminus of the line on the opposite side of the River Wyre to Fleetwood, at half past eleven in the morning, and were taken to Garstang and Catterall Station, where the new line makes a junction with the London and North Western main line. The new line is four and a half miles long and the approximate cost of its construction has been between £35,000 and £40,000. It has presented no engineering difficulties, the track being throughout as near perfectly level as possible, and there is but one bridge, which has only a span of sixteen feet. The new railway will open out and develop one of the most fertile agricultural areas in the county which has not up to the present had any railway facilities. By means of the extension, Fleetwood, Blackpool and other Fylde seaside resorts will be in close touch with a large population which has hitherto been attached to Morecambe."*

The antiquated carriages and rolling were to be disposed of and new engines and carriages were provided. The engines were both supplied by Manning and Wardle of Leeds. "Knott End" was a 0-6-0 side tank that was delivered late 1908 and "Blackpool" a 2-6-0 side tank in 1909. Eight new carriages, each capable of carrying 50 passengers, were ordered from the Birmingham Waggon Company. The old railway had been worked without signals. Under the new regime there was proper signaling equipment, and telephonic communication between all the stations.

So, after receiving the Royal Assent for the bill to construct the line on the 30th June, 1864, the line was finally completed 44 years later. Most of the original directors and shareholders had long since died and the circumstances for the purpose of the railway had changed. There would never be a dock at Knott End, nor a connection to the ports on the east coast. Transport was changing, with road transport starting to seriously complete with the railways. The companies had purchased enough land to change the single line into a double one, but it was never needed. Instead the extra land in places was used for a hay crop and in others allotments were rented out to local people. A 1908 penny guide to the railway said "Leaving Pilling station by train, we observe that the superfluous land on the line has been let as garden plots to cottagers, the railway being flanked on either side by fine displays of flowers and vegetables."

The picture is of Knott End taking on water, probably at Garstang. On the next page is a timetable for July and August, 1908, the first one for the complete line. G Errol Worthington is the general manager. On the following page is a postcard showing a charabanc which had been running since 1904. The start of the competition.

KNOTT END RAILWAY.

TIME TABLE FOR JULY & AUGUST, 1908, AND UNTIL FURTHER NOTICE.

Up

Miles	STATIONS		1 a.m. B	2 a.m. A	3 a.m.	4 p.m.	5 p.m.	6 p.m.	7 p.m.	8 p.m. *	9 p.m. A	10 p.m. Not on Saturdays	11 p.m. Saturdays only	12
0	Knott End	depart	7 30	9 25	11 15	12 15	1 52	5 24	3 54	6 7	5	3 09	7 10	2 10
1	Preesall	"	7 36	9 31	11 21	12 21	1 58	5 27	3 59	9 5	5 27	3 69	1 3 10	7 10
4¼	Pilling	"	7 45	9 40	11 25	12 30	2 30	3 03	7 4	1 56	17 4	3 39	2 2 10	1 7 10
7½	Nateby	"	5 5	9 45	...	12 35	...	...	4 2	66 9	...	3 0	10 25	12 3 38
9½	Garstang	"	09 55	9 55	...	12 45	2 40	5 40 3	4 33	6 16	...	3 37	10 32	10 30 12 43
11¼	Garstang & Catterall	arr	5 10 3	10 3	...	12 53	...	...	4 41	6 24	...	3 45	10 40	10 38

	Depart for Preston		8 16	10 14	...	1 12	12 45	...	5 5	6 20	4 35	...	...	...
	Arrive at Preston		8 38	10 35	...	1 35	1 12	...	5 30	6 54	5 5	...	...	...
	Depart for Lancaster		08 30	10 9	...	1 1	12 42	...	4 40	...	4 30	9 54	10 50	...
	Arrive at Lancaster		08 59	10 34	...	1 26	1 7	...	5 14	...	4 49	10 15	11 10	...

SUNDAYS.

	1 a.m.	2 a.m.	3	4 p.m.	5 p.m.	6 p.m.	7 p.m.	8 p.m.
Knott End				3 04	5 05	4 07		08 47
Preesall				3 64	5 65	4 67		68 53
Pilling				4 55	4 33	5 57	3 5	15 9 2
Nateby				3 53	6	37	2 39	10
Garstang				3 58	6	87	3 09	15
Garstang & Catterall					7	38		

| | | | | | | 7 45 |
| | | | | | | 8 13 |

Down

Miles	STATIONS		1 a.m.	2 a.m.	3	4 a.m.	5	6 p.m.	7 p.m.	8 p.m.	9 A	10 p.m.	11 p.m.	12 Not on Saturdays	13 Saturdays only
0	Garstang & Catterall	dp		8 32 10	9 46 16	1 14	5	76 31					8 42	9 55 10 55	
2	Garstang	"	6 408	4 2 10	10 26	1 24 2	1 82 524	65 176 41					0 33	10 3 11 3	10 30
4	Nateby	"	6 468	4 8 10	10 32	1 30 2	58	5 236 47					0 39	10 50	
7	Pilling	"	6 558	5 7 10	4 11 1	39 2	30 303 74	185 326 568					9 51		
10	Preesall	"	49	6 10	50 11	4 51	39 2 482 393	275 417 58							
11¼	Knott End	arrive	7 89	10 10	54 11	4 91	1 522 433	315 457 98							

SUNDAYS.

	1 a.m.	2 a.m.	13 p.m.	1 p.m.	2 p.m.	3 p.m.	4 p.m.	5 p.m.	6 p.m.	7 p.m.	8 p.m.
Garstang & Catterall	8 9	9	10 50		12 53		4 8			6 20	7 47
Garstang	9 15	11	10	11	6 12 59		4 14	5 15		6 26	7 57
Nateby	9 21 1	11	11	15 1	8 3 0		4 23	5 24		6 35	8 3
Pilling	9 30 11	11 24 1		17	23		4 32	5 28		6 44	8 12
Preesall	9 39 11	11 28 1		21 3 13			4 36			6 48	8 21
Knott End	9 43 11										8 25

| | | | | | 7 15 |
| | | | | | 7 45 |

1 Stops at Cogie Hill and Cockerham Cross on Thursdays and Saturdays when required.
B. Stops at Cogie Hill and Cockerham Cross on Saturdays when required.
C Leaves Garstang & Catterall 8 14 a.m., and arrives at Lancaster at 8 31 a.m. on Saturdays and Mondays.

G. ERROLL WORTHINGTON, Manager.

OFFICES—KNOTT END, LANCASHIRE.   R. WRIGHTSON, PRINTER AND STATIONER, POST OFFICE MARKET PLACE, GARSTANG.

Running Daily during the Season. KNOT END and PILLING, FARE 6d. EACH WAY.

Fleetwood Motor Passenger Carrying Co., Ltd., Fleetwood.

Over the next four pages are simple drawings of the engines used on the Garstang and Knott End Railway. They are not meant to be accurate, technical line drawings, but are merely intended to give an idea of how the engines looked. The names and lettering on the drawings are only included for identification purpose and are not meant to represent the actual position used at the time. Some technical details of each engine are included, along with their final destinations, where known.

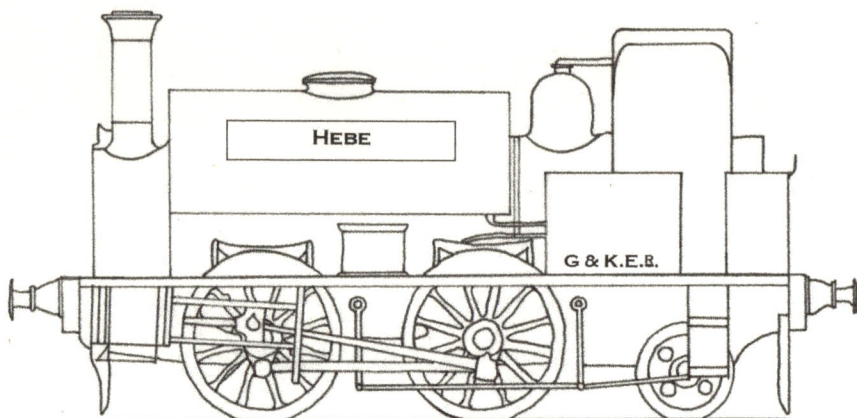

Hebe was the first engine on the line. It was an 0-4-2 saddle tank, built in 1870 by Black, Hawthorne & Co, of Gateshead. The coupled wheels were 3ft 6ins in diameter with a pair of trailing wheels 2ft 6ins in diameter. The wheelbase was 5ft 6ins by 5ft. The outside cylinders were 13ins by 18ins, driving the rear coupled axle. The boiler was small with a total heating surface of 321 square feet, and a working pressure of 12 lb. The saddle tank covered the boiler and held 400 gallons. The rear bunker provided space for 15cwt. of coal. The cab was little more than a roof supported by front and back weatherboards. The only brake was hand operated and connected to wooden blocks at the rear of the coupled wheels. The engine, after being taken out of service in 1872 for repairs, was taken back by the owners for non-payment of the instalments. After being taken back from The Garstang & Knot End Railway it went to a J P Radley, then Lea Green Colliery and about 1998 to T Mitchell of Bolton, a dealer.

Union was the second engine on the line, purchased second hand in 1875 from James Pilling, a contractor, who had built the Lancashire Union Railway. It was manufactured by Manning, Wardle & Company of Leeds in 1868. It was an 0-4-0 saddle tank. The wheels were 2ft 9ins in diameter on a 5ft wheelbase. The cylinders were 9½ins by 14ins. The boiler had a heating surface of 319 square feet and the saddle tank held 350 gallons. Side bunkers held 15cwt. of coal. There was no cab fitted, only a front weatherboard. It was part-exchanged in 1884 for another engine and shortly afterwards was at the Fleetwood Salt Company and in 1998 went to Wilson Lovatt & Sons Ltd, a firm of contractors.

Farmers' Friend was delivered in 1875. It was an 0-6-0 saddle tank engine supplied by Hudswell, Clarke & Co. The wheels were 3 feet in diameter on a 10 feet 6 ins wheelbase. The cylinders were 11ins by 17ins. The boiler was 3 feet in diameter, 8 feet 4ins in length and worked at 120lbs pressure. The saddle tank held 500 gallons. A sheet iron roof covered the footplate and the bunker. Farmer's Friend went back to Hudswell Clarke in 1897 in part exchange for a new engine and was sold to J F Howard, of Bedford, about 1900.

Hope was purchased in 1884 from Hudswell, Clarke and Company. It was an 0-6-0 saddle tank engine similar but a little larger than Farmers' Friend. It had a cab roof with curved weatherboards. The cylinders were 13ins by 20ins and the wheels were 3 feet 6ins on a 12 feet wheelbase. The boiler was 3 feet in diameter and 9 feet 6ins long giving a total of 464 square feet of heating area. The saddle tank water capacity was 500 gallons and the bunker held a ton and a half of coal. There was a hand brake working iron blocks on the wheels. Hope was taken back in 1900 and sold to T Mitchell of Bolton, a dealer.

Jubilee Queen and New Century were more or less identical. They were 0-6-0 saddle tank engines from Hudswell, Clarke and Company. Jubilee Queen purchased in 1897 and New Century in 1900. Their outside cylinders were 15ins by 20ins, the wheels 3 feet 6ins diameter with a 12 feet wheelbase. The boilers were 3 feet 5ins diameter and 9 feet 3ins long with 660 square feet of heating surface. The saddle tank held 750 gallons water and the bunker one and a half tons of coal. There was a full cab fitted. The engines had hand and steam brakes. Jubilee Queen was scrapped at Crewe in March, 1926 and New Century was scrapped in November, 1925.

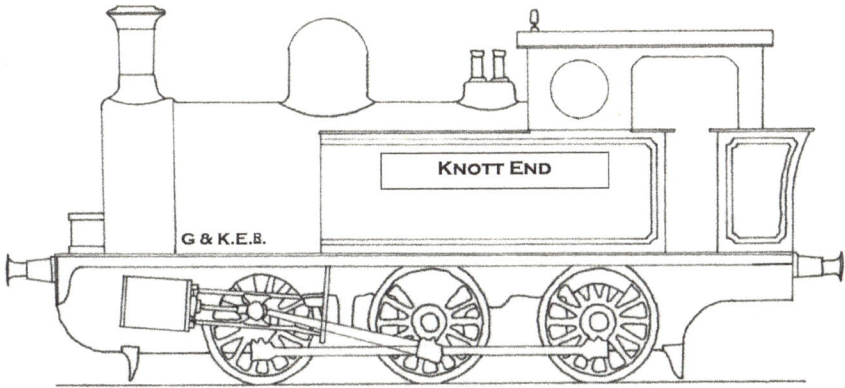

Knott End was purchased in 1908 from Manning, Wardle and Company, of Leeds, and was an 0-6-0 side tank engine. The cylinders were outside and were 14ins by 20ins. The wheels were 3 feet 9ins in diameter on a 10 feet 6ins wheelbase. The boiler was 3 feet 11ins diameter and 8 feet long and had a heating surface of 610 square feet. The side tanks held 700 gallons of water and the bunker one and a half tons of coal. Vacuum brakes were fitted during manufacture. In 1923 Knott End was allotted L.M.S. number 11302 and was scrapped at Horwich in June. 1924.

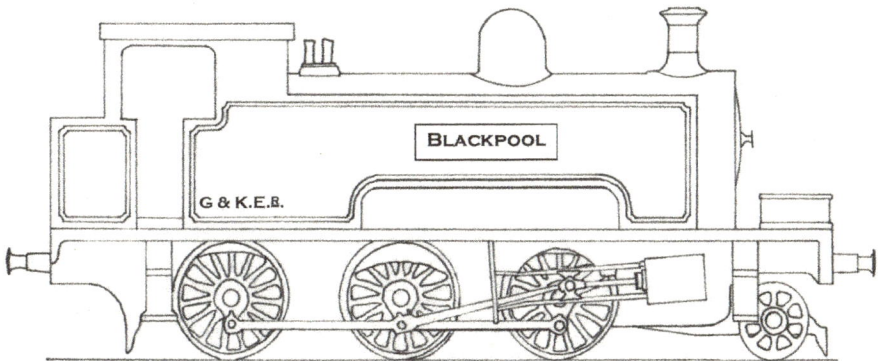

Blackpool was a 2-6-0 side tank engine purchased from Manning, Wardle and Company in 1909. It was the largest engine the company ever had and was intended for goods traffic. The coupled wheels were 4 feet in diameter and the leading wheels 2 feet 9½ins. The wheelbase was 20 feet 9ins. The outside cylinders were 16ins by 22ins and the boiler was 4 feet 5ins in diameter with a length of 10 feet. It had a 832 square feet heating surface and worked at 150 lbs pressure. The tanks carried 1000 gallons of water and the bunker held 2 tons of coal. It was overhauled and painted at Crewe in 1924 and was scrapped in October, 1927.

Knott End locomotive at Knott End station with the Bourne Arms visible in the background. A postcard published by the Locomotive Publishing Company.

Knott End locomotive again at Knott End station all steamed up with a full load of carriages all ready to go. From an old postcard, unknown publisher.

In the Railway World Magazine of July, 1958 is a description of the new coaches.

"The new engine Knott End came down from the junction with a train of eight handsome new corridor coaches each with a capacity of 50 seats. These were indeed rather fine vehicles of plenteous dimensions. At first glance they were something of the order of the American pattern bogie cars. Like their predecessors, they had seating on either side of a central gangway, and balconies roofed over, ornamental railings round the ends, and gates to the balconies. There were steps for mounting from the track side and the first class had curtains to the windows. The whole of each side was glazed. The bogies had both axlebox and large transverse springs and were fitted with vacuum brakes, the line until then having satisfied itself with hand brakes on passenger trains. The bogie wheels were unusual in that they had spokes. At this period all stock was painted brown."

The total cost to the Knott End Railway Company came to £179,991, which broke down as £19,065 for the uncompleted extension of 1898, and £44,690 to finish the work to 1908. For the purchase of The Garstang and Knot End Railway and its rolling stock together with the new locomotive, eight carriages, six wagons and three brake vans, £110,000. There was also a charge of £5,000 for shares and £1,236 in legal and other charges. The length of the extension was 4 miles 32 chains (a chain is 22 yards).

Adverts were placed, by the Garstang and Knot End Railway Company, in the press in August, 1908 asking that any creditors make any claims or demands for debts incurred be sent to the liquidators of the company by 24 September, 1908. They were also requesting shareholders to make a claim to participate in the division of £5,000 shares in The Knott End Railway Company.

By 1909 the company was auctioning off old stock including two third class carriages, two composite corridor (first and third class) carriages plus a large amount of hardware.

In 1910 an action took place at St George's Hall, Liverpool regarding the purchase money obtained by the Garstang and Knot End Railway in 1908. It concerned the share out of the money. It was said that Mr William Gilbertson acted as solicitor for the company and he also hired out to the company the rolling stock used on the line consisting of an engine, four passenger carriages, and twenty five goods wagons. In this transaction other persons were interested. In the years 1882,1883 and 1884 he brought an action against the company in respect of the sums due to him. He received judgement for amounts aggregating £1,300 for services as solicitor, £802 for the hire of the passenger carriages, £627 for the hire of the engine and £1,775 for the hire of the wagons. This money was never received until after the purchase of the company by the Knott End Railway when a total of £4,411 was paid To Mr W R Gilbertson as the legal representative of Mr William Gilbertson. The defendants were the executors of George Bush (the contractor who built the line), Robert Green Watson, James Hamilton and John Hamilton who claimed a portion of the pay out as joint owners of the rolling stock. An inquiry was ordered as to the apportionment of the funds.

The Knott End extension had been built with the United Alkali Company in mind, which had a large works at Preesall, where a large area of land was given over to the mining of brine deposits. The brine mining was carried out by the Fleetwood Salt Company who leased 445 hectares of land close to Preesall and a further 9 hectares at Burn Naze for the works.

The brine mining had started seriously in 1875 with an eight foot diameter borehole sunk by the Reverend Daniels and Daniel Elletson. By 1885 the borehole was over 600 feet deep and the brine was carried across the river by a pipeline. The first white salt was produced at Burn Naze in 1890 and the company was sold to the United Alkali Company in 1891.

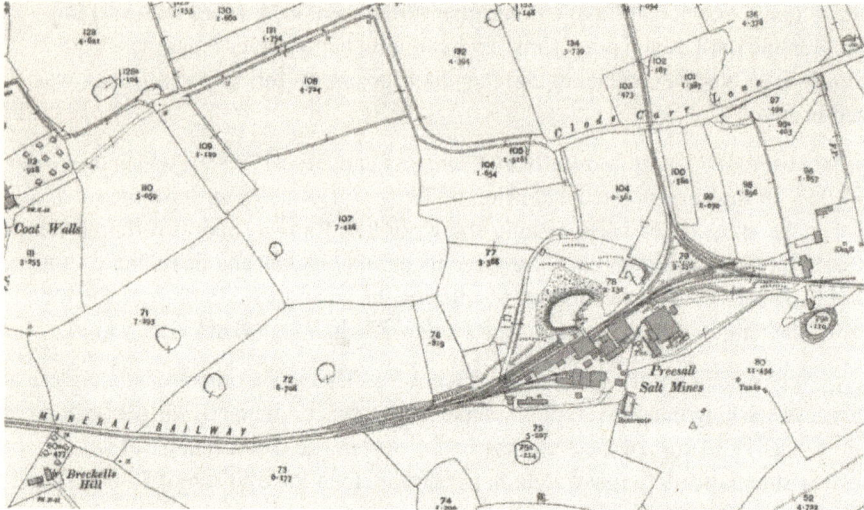

Preesal Salt Mine Works. The railway goes west to a jetty on the River Wyre and north to join the Knott End Railway.

Around 1902, Preesall Salt Works was built to the north of the salt marshes. A branch line was built to the Knott End Railway in 1912. In 1909 55 tons of salt were carried on the railway. After the mineral line was opened in 1912, the amount was 2,241 tons carried by the railway. By 1913 it was 7,916 tons and in 1920 the total salt carried was 53,416 tons. Also the works required large amounts of coal; 13,663 tons in 1913 and 24,135 in 1920.

Another product which helped the profitability of the railway was moss litter. This was one of the main natural products of the district and was used mainly for horse and cattle bedding. 2,117 ton was carried in 1913 reaching a peak in 1916 of 6,854 tons. The carriage of beer told a different story. From a peak of 356 in 1909 it fell, because the brewers suppling the district gradually moved to motor traction, to a low of one ton in 1920.

At a meeting of the shareholders held at the company offices in Knott End in March, 1915, the net revenue was £1,138. The chairman, Mr John Patterson said that the goods traffic was the only department of the company's undertaking that paid. They made nothing out of passengers, whom they simply carried to oblige.

A halt was added at Carr Lane, on the Knott End Extension, in 1911 and another one was made at Garstang Road, half a mile on the east side of Pilling. Cockerham Cross and Cogie Hill, previously referred to as pick up places on market days, had become regular halts. The train service, in 1911, consisted of three trains in each direction between Knott End and Garstang and Catterall plus a morning one from Garstang to the main line, and a return one in the evening from Knott End to Garstang.

The Grouping of Railways Act of 1919-1920 gave the Knott End Railway Company to the London, Midland & Scottish Railway and it then became just a small part of a large company. The final settlement was in 1923 and the Knott End shareholders got 125 shillings of L.M.S. ordinary stock for every £100 of Knott End stock. Compared to 1913, the last complete year of the accounts in 1922 showed a reduction in passengers from 91,918 to 77,579, an increase in goods from 19,033 tons to 69,535 tons and an increase in revenue from £1,179 to £1,232.

In 1920 the goods traffic of the railway meant that most of the locomotives were needed for the wagons and a steam rail motor, seating 48 third class passengers, was hired from the L.& N.W. Railway. This was used until the end of passenger services. During the twenties there was a rapid growth in road transport, which led to the decision to close the railway for passenger traffic. On the 10th March, 1930, an announcement was made that the passenger train service on the Garstang and Catterall-Knott End would be withdrawn on the 1st April. Passenger traffic in the area served by the line would be diverted to a motor bus system, which was already in operation and would be extended to Catterall for travel by mail line trains.

Mr J E N Ashworth visited the line for the final journey for the "Railway Magazine" and there was an account in the June, 1930 issue. He obtained the last return ticket issued from Knott End for the whole of the line. The ex L.N.W.R. motor train, which had worked most of the passenger traffic on the line for several years, was in attendance. As this was the last trip there were numerous passengers collected at each stop and the train was full by the time it reached Garstang Town. There the crew was changed and most of the passengers exited the train. It then left for Garstang and Catterall station where the train ran into a bay on the outer side of the down main line platform. Passenger traffic had been scanty for a long time with Garstang being on a main road well served by buses. Knott End was a small seaside resort, but most people travelled to it by ferry from Fleetwood. The train service consisted of five trains on weekdays only in each direction (six in summer), and two extra ones in either direction between the town station and the junction with the main line. The average time taken was 38 minutes to cover the 11½ miles. The average time taken by the bus service was 50 minutes. Garstang, Nateby, Pilling, Preesall and Knott End stations would remain open for Parcels and goods traffic but the halts would be closed. The goods line to the salt works at Preesall was to remain open.

"The return journey from Garstang and Catterall to Knott End was the last through trip in this direction. We left with a fair complement of passengers, with the whistle working overtime. At Garstang Town the train was filled up, and we left amidst more whistling, to the accompaniment of numerous fog signals. The journey to Knott End was uneventful; at all the level crossings people were waving, and there were fog signals on

the track at various places. At last we arrived at the terminus, and I stayed on the platform to see the last train depart from Knott End. It rounded the curve, and then all that could be seen was a cloud of steam. A few minutes later, as I made my way down to the ferry boat, the engine's whistle could again be heard 'crowing,' and the bangs of two fog signals indicated the departure of the last passenger train from Preesall station."

In the evening a farewell dinner was held at the Royal Oak, Garstang. This function was described as like a funeral feast in honour of the "Pilling Pig." Mr Whalley, while proposing a toast for the staff, expressed regret that the line had been closed, and ventured the opinion that the authorities had made a profound mistake. He predicted that the line would be re-opened for passengers. One of the guests was Mr J Alston, formerly secretary and manager of the line, who joined the company in 1875 as it started up again after the closure in 1872. Another guest was Mr G E Worthington, the son of the contractor for the Knott End extension, who was a former general manager. He said the best year on the line was 1920, when 112,00 passengers were carried. On August Bank Holiday, 1909, they had a record day. Between the hours of 11a.m. and 6 p.m. they had a train in and out of Knott End every 15 minutes.

TO be Let, the undermentioned Station Buildings and Premises, formerly used in connection with the Garstang and Knott End Railway:

Garstang Town.—Carriage Shed and Engine Shed; large corrugated iron buildings; two Waiting Rooms, on platform, with lavatory accommodation.

Cogie Hill Halt.—Wooden Waiting Room.

Pilling.—Two Waiting Rooms, Booking Hall, and Booking Office.

Carr-lane Halt.—Wooden Waiting Room.

Preesall.—Waiting Room.

Knott End.—Waiting Room, Booking Hall, Station Master's Office, and Booking Office.

For particulars apply, T. KITTSON, I.M.S. Railway, District Estate Office, 10, Walton's-parade, Preston.

The mineral branch line to Preesall salt works closed in 1934 and was removed. Also at this time a moss litter plant, near Cogie Hill, closed thus reducing the amount of goods carried by the railway. During the second world war the cutting to the east of Garstang Town was used twice by the Royal Train as a safe overnight stopping place. On the 13th November, 1950, the section from Pilling to Knott End was closed and shortly afterwards the track was lifted and the land was put up for sale. Nateby station was also closed down at this time. A man with many memories was Mr Tom Langley, of Preesall, who was guard on the first train from Knott End, and the station master on the last.

The line from Pilling to Garstang was closed on the 31st July, 1963 and was reported in the Fleetwood Chronicle.

"Railway engine 45390, pulling a dozen wagons puffed out of Pilling station at 3.20 p.m. last Wednesday on its way to Garstang, the last train to use the line which has been axed by Dr. Beeching. About 50 people waved goodbye as the driver, James Cox, of Waverley Road, Preston, who has made the trip for more than 20 years, blew a farewell blast on the engine's whistle. Among those watching the train off was Mrs Dorothy Dickinson, of Holly Bank, Pilling, whose home adjoins the station. She had watched the daily train arrive and leave for more than 20 years."

The line was closed to all traffic in August, 1965

*   *   *   *

Incidents and Accidents

Lancaster Gazette 30/10/1869

On Monday afternoon, a labourer, named Thomas Topping, of Preston, employed on the Garstang and Knot End Railway was knocked down by a wagon laden with earth, as it was being run down to a tip. The wagon passed over him, and nearly severed his right leg at the thigh, and he died in about 15 minutes.

Lancaster Gazette 25/03/1871

On Friday the 10th, at the Stakepool station of the Garstang and Knot End line, an accident occured. A farmer, of the name of Ralph Mason, who with his horse and cart, had some business there, was engaged about the station, when the horse, frightened by the noise of the train, suddenly became restive. and ran the cart against a wagon, when the deceased, William Percy, was caught between the cart and the buffer of the railway wagon, and was so severely crushed that he died immediately. At the inquest in March, 1872, Margaret Turner, of Pilling, said that William Percy was her father and was 79 years old and a shoemaker. Richard Thornton, of Nateby, a contractor, said that he knew Mr Percy. The wagons were being loaded with potatoes, but he had nothing to do with the loading. Richard Smith, of Garstang, was the engine driver and he said that he had seen Mr Percy standing on the side of the railway but when he pushed the carriages by the engine towards where he was standing the line was clear. Edward Skeffington, general manager of the railway, said that the deceased had no business of his own to transact on the railway on Friday, and he had warned him several times not to go near the trains. The verdict was accidently killed.

Lancaster Gazette 16/03/1872

On Saturday afternoon last, a fatal accident occurred on the Garstang and Knot End Railway to the clerk, John Armistead Shakleton. The deceased, along with a labourer, was engaged in shunting a carriage, aided by the engine. The engine was on the mail line, and the carriage to be shunted was on the siding. Shackleton got a long pole and held it to the end of the engine with the other end against the carriage. Whilst shunting in this manner the end of the pole next to the carriage slipped and the deceased being in the middle of the line of rails the engine came on , and he was crushed to death. Robert Laird, the engine driver, was on dinner and the stoker, James Sturzaker, was driving the engine.

Preston Chronicle 27/11/1875

A shocking and fatal accident occurred at the level crossing on the Garstang and Knot End Railway, on Monday night last, to a man named John Graystone. George Graystone, of Nateby, labourer, said the deceased was his son, and was 34 years of age, and was a farm labourer. He had been engaged with him during the day collecting tolls at Wyre Bridge, and left about a quarter to five. He had not had much drink, only a squib or two, and something from the bottle when at the bridge collecting tolls. Deceased called for a pair of clogs at Benson's for his child. When we arrived at the level crossing at the back of the town, the gates were shut, and we went though a side gate on the line, and deceased said he would go down the line as far as Sandwell's crossing. Immediately after, when we had got about six yards from the gate, the train came up and knocked him down. Assistance then came, and he was carried into the station, and Drs Chapman and Dewhurst were sent for. He was much mashed about the thighs, and died about a quarter to ten o'clock. Joseph Hodgkinson was the driver of the engine.

Preston Chronicle 19/03/1881

On Saturday afternoon, James William Salisbury, stoker on the Farmer's Friend, an engine on the Garstang and Knot End Railway, met with a serious accident. The engine was engaged in shunting, and the man was getting between two wagons to uncouple them, when they commenced moving. He tried to get from between them, when he was knocked down and one of the wagons passed over the thigh of his right leg, fracturing it severely. He was taken to Dr. Irvine, who attended to his injuries, after which he was conveyed to the Preston Infirmary. He is reported to be progressing satisfactorily.

Preston Chronicle 24/09/1887

As the midday train from Pilling was proceeding to Garstang and was only a short distance away, a donkey was noticed on the track. When the train drew near the donkey refused to move and it was killed on the spot. The animal had strayed out of a field on the line, and was the property of John Hoole, farmer, Winmarleigh.

Lancaster Gazette 25/01/1890

On Friday week a labourer living at Barnacre, named Cooper, and another man, were returning home from Garstang, and walked along the line of the Knot End Railway. It was dark at the time at the time, and in crossing a cattle creep Cooper missed his footing and fell over, a depth of about twenty feet. His companion went to Skirrington Hall, obtained assistance, and the injured man was conveyed there. Dr Gorham was called in the following day and found Cooper much hurt, several of his ribs being broken. He attended him until Thursday at noon, when he expired.

Preston Herald 15/02/1890

At the Preston Infimary, on Thursday, an inquest was held by the Coroner upon the body of Robert Bradshaw, a potato dealer, of Fisher's Road, Pilling. (see page 68).

Preston Herald 19/07/1890

Still another serious accident has to be reported through the nightly custom of walking along the Garstang and Knot End Railway in the dark. On wednesday night, between eleven and twelve o'clock, a couple of pipe track labourers were walking along the line from Garstang in the direction of Barnacre, when one of them, named Robert Clarke-known as Nobby Clarke-fell over Cattle Creep Bridge (which is without parapet) into the field below, a distance of about 20 feet. The man lay where he fallen until Thursday morning, when his companion saw Mr Barton, relieving officer, and was given an order for the workhouse for Clarke. The man was then conveyed to the house by Mr Isles, of the Royal Oak Hotel, where it was found he had sustained a severe shaking and injury to the ribs.

Preston Chronicle 28/03/1891

At a vestry meeting of the ratepayers of the township of Barnacre-with-Bonds, held on Monday at the house of Mr Edward Southworth, the Kenlis Arms Hotel, it was resolved to present a requisition to the Garstang and Knot End Railway, praying them to adopt some efficient means of protection against a recurrence of the sad, fatal and distressing accidents which have from time to time occurred at a bridge on the line, called Greenhalgh Castle Creep.

Preston Herald 22/08/1903

The sudden death occurred on Monday of a platelayer named Thomas Greenwood, who was taken ill whilst working on the line near the Garstang and Knot End Railway Station. He was taken to his home and medical assistance summoned but he succumbed suddenly. Deceased was 70 years of age and was well known in the district.

Lancashire Evening Post 09/11/1906

During the storm of yesterday afternoon Mr William Wilkinson, of Hunter's Farm, Pilling, a well known farmer, was walking on the Garstang and Knot End Railway line at Pilling when he was caught by an engine. One of his feet was badly crushed.

Northern Daily Telegraph 20/02/1909

The engine shed at Garstang Station on the Garstang and Knott End Railway, was destroyed by fire early yesterday morning. It was discovered by two engine cleaners, named Chippendal and Swarbrick. Three engines that were in the shed were got out.

Lieutenant Noel Trevor Worthington, 6th Battalion, King's Own Royal Lancs Regiment

Noel and his brother George Errol Worthington were the sons of Robert Worthington, of Salmon Poole, Dublin and the great grandsons of Sir William Worthington, Lord Mayor of Dublin in 1795-6. Robert Worthington was the contractor who completed the extension of the line to Knott End. His sons came over to run the railway and George was the general manager and Noel was the assistant manager and secretary. He volunteered for war service in August,1914 and was trained in Wiltshire and Aldershot. He was sent to Gallipoli and arrived in August, 1915. He landed at a place called Suvla Bay and was in charge of the grenadier company of his regiment and had only been there for a couple of days when the Turkish attacked them and Lieutenant Noel Worthington was posted as wounded and then missing believed killed. It was reported that he fell while rallying his men when attacked by overwhelming numbers. He is buried at Embarkation Pier Cemetery, near Chailak Dere, Turkey.

His brother Lieutenant G Errol Worthington served with the Army Service Corps. He was a guest at the farewell dinner for the last passenger service, held at the Royal Oak, Garstang, in 1930.

Bibliography

The Garstang and Knott End Railway. R W Rush and M R C Price. 1985.

Knott End and Preesall, the story of a township. Martin Ramsbottom 1993

Northwards. Andrew Hewitson. 1900

Victoria County History of Lancashire. 1912

Pigot and Co's Directory of Cumberland, Lancashire and Westmoreland. 1828-9.

Garstang's Great War Heroes. Paul Smith and Anthony Coppin. 2016.

Railway Magazine, Jan 1908, Dec 1924, June 1930, Dec 1959.

Railway World, July 1958.

Garstang and Knott End Railway. Margaret Edwards. 1973

Thanks to Bob Dobson of Landy Publishing for the loan of some original documents.

The files of the Preston Chronicle, Preston Herald and Lancaster Gazette.

All map clips Crown Copyright.